Lectures on Tibetan Medicine

by
Lady Doctor
Lobsang Dolma Khangkar

Compiled and edited by
K. Dhondup

LIBRARY OF TIBETAN WORKS & ARCHIVES

Copyright © 1986: Library of Tibetan Works and Archives

First Print 1986
Second Print 1991
Third (Revised) 1998
This Edition 2009

ALL RIGHTS RESERVED

No part of this publication may be reproduced, stored in a retrieval system, or transmitted in any form or by any means, electronic, mechanical, photo-copying, recording or otherwise, without the prior permission of the publisher.

ISBN: 978-81-86470-94-7

Published by the Library of Tibetan Works and Archives, Dharamsala, H.P. 176215, and printed at Indraprastha Press (CBT), Nehru House, New Delhi-110002

Publisher's Note

As it is the aim of the Library of Tibetan Works & Archives to preserve and promote all the aspects of the Tibetan cultural and literary traditions, we are happy to publish a compilation of the lectures by Dr. Dolma on Tibetan Medicine.

We are sure that these lectures will be useful to the students and physicians of the Tibetan medical system and the increasing number of non-Tibetan students who have a strong and sincere interest in the various cures propounded by the Tibetan physicians for a number of chronic ailments.

Gyatsho Tshering
Director
March 1998

Preface

I have always wanted to compile Dr. Dolma's lectures on Tibetan medicine and publish them under one cover. As her son-in-law, I have had easy access to the tapes and typescripts of her lectures translated by different translators at different times in different countries. For this compilation, I have drawn mainly from the lectures at Kolmas in Holland where Dr. Dolma gave a month-long course after attending the first International Conference on Tibetan Medicine at Milan in Italy. I have also drawn from her Australian lectures where she attended the International Conference on Traditional Asian Medicine at the University of Canberra and spoke extensively on different aspects of Tibetan medicine to appreciative audiences everywhere. Whenever and wherever it was possible and necessary, I have personally consulted Dr. Dolma for corrections, clarifications and textual references. Yet in work of such a nature where much remains to be translated and interpreted in western medical terminology, many theories and concepts are still unclear and mistakes of interpretation and translations remain. For such drawbacks in this edition, I judge myself personally responsible.

As she was always involved with the task of relieving the distress of the patients, Dr. Dolma had neither the time nor the energy to sit for long hours of discussion on a particular aspect of Tibetan medicine. Frankly speaking, she considers the treatment of patients as the most important field of her work as a doctor. In her dedication to her profession and in her compassion for the sick and the suffering patients, she gave no importance to a compilation and publication of her lectures on Tibetan medicine. It was with some difficulty that I finally succeeded in getting her full consent to bring out the present edition. Though many of the chapters have been re-written and edited after careful consultation with Dr. Dolma, I have tried to keep the essence and original flavour of the lectures, as well as the question and answer sessions that followed the lectures. Suggestions and criticisms from the readers, especially the Tibetan medical community, are always welcome.

Dr. Dolma is a great doctor. Not because she is my mother-in-law, but because she is one of the most magnificent manifestations of the compassionate and selfless Buddhist physicians to whom relieving the pains and suffering of the patients acquire the greatest importance above anything else. Those who have closely observed her during her working hours will attest to the sublime dedication with which she uploads her profession, and the sincerity and compassion with which she applies her immense skill and knowledge of her art to dispel the psychological and physical stress and distress of her patients. Observing Dr. Dolma in action makes the fact clear that knowledge and skill by themselves are not enough to become a good doctor. Love, kindness and compassion towards the patients and a sincere effort to share their hardship is an equal—if not more—important and essential quality of a doctor. Dr. Dolma has both the qualities in ample measure.

Today Tibetan medicine is popular. With a little more effort, it is destined to relieve the sickness and suffering of millions throughout the world. For Tibetan medicine to become such a healing force, more and more doctors must be trained, not only in the traditional medical science itself, but also in the allied sciences of allopathy and other alternative disciplines. This way, Tibetan doctors can combine their traditional skills with the scientific urge to discover and create new skills that can take up the challenge of curing the psychological and physical ailments of our violent times. For this to happen, the small community of the Tibetan doctors must themselves shed their shell and come out in the open to form a professional community, exchange and enrich their medical ideas and thereby develop an honest sense of appreciation and respect for each other. Only then can this ancient healing science of Tibet become a force that can contribute something substantial and lasting the world. If in the name of preserving culture, doctors remain chained to an insensitive and mediocre bureaucracy without getting the respect and freedom that they deserve, Tibetan medicine will die a natural death. Once in a while, one doctor or another may become a little famous and have a flourishing practice. Though praiseworthy, this will not be a lasting Tibetan contribution to humanity itself. For that to happen, doctors must have the social and economic respect and freedom to practice their art and refine their skill in a way that is beneficial both to themselves, to their community and to the human society at large.

Tibetan medicine, in theory, is complicated, intriguing and almost pseudo-scientific with its many mythological and religious references. However, in practice, it is simple, convenient and almost scientific. The patient sits in front of the doctor who examines the pulse. If the patient had brought his or her urine, it is also examined. Some questions are asked. According to the reading of the pulse, the urine sample and the answers of the patient, the patient's problem is identified. A medication is prescribed. Some precautions relating to diet and behavior, etc. are given and there ends the scene. No complicated, time consuming, expensive or even painful tests are performed. If a week's medicine is of some help, the patient is advised to continue with the same medication. If it has been of no help, a fresh pulse and other examinations are made and the prescription of the medication undergoes the necessary changes. In this simple way, the treatment continues. Through such an uncomplicated and convenient treatment, many have been cured of chronic diseases like asthma, arthritis, diabetes, ulcer and even cancer, to mention a few. Such a science, so simple yet so secret, has something more to contribute to the world. It is for the Tibetan doctors to take up the initiative and share this almost unique system of healing with the rest of humanity.

Yet sharing this skill of healing with others will be truly challenging. No one, least of all the medical community that exists outside the Tibetan cultural world, will welcome it with open arms. In fact, it will be heard with skepticism and observed with the most analytic, if not negative and condescending attitude by both the lay and professional non-Tibetan medical community. In Holland, Dr. Dolma successfully treated a girl who was suffering from epilepsy. When her parents took the girl to her own doctors who had diagnosed her as epileptic and given up her case as hopeless and incurable, the doctors, instead of appreciating and welcoming the girl patient's remarkable response to Tibetan medicine as prescribed by Dr. Dolma, went back on their original diagnosis and claimed they may have made a mistake in diagnosing the girl as epileptic since, according to them, epilepsy is incurable. This is just one example. In our time of extreme cynicism, Tibetan medicine and doctors will face many uncomfortable challenges of doubt and suspicion. They must overcome such crises of faith and healing with their medical skill and spiritual wisdom. For example, either surprised or shocked by the cures of Tibetan medicine, many wrongly whisper that a strong allopathic drug is being secretly mixed with the Tibetan pills which apparently adds the curative power that has miraculously cured many chronic cases. This accusation may be out of genuine concern. It may also be professional jealousy. Whatever the case, the Tibetan doctors must be prepared to stand up to the challenge of demonstrating their skill and cures to those that are interested in it. They have everything to win. My personal experience of involvement with Tibetan medicine gives me enough courage to state that Tibetan medicine is among the most useful sciences that mankind presently has.

K. Dhondup
April, 1986

Contents

Publisher's Note		iii
Preface		v
1	Introduction	1
2	History and Origin of Tibetan Medicine	4
3	The Four Tantras	8
4	The Training of the Tibetan Doctor	16
5	The Three Humors	20
6	The Functions of the Three Humors	30
7	Relationship Between Body, Speech and Mind	37
8	Rebirth	46
9	Buddhism and Medicine	51
10	Diagnosis in Practice	66
11	Child Conception	73
12	Massage	102
13	Breathing Exercises	107
14	The Spleen and its Functions	112
15	Tibetan Medical Concept of Insanity	119
16	Theory of Diagnosis	124
17	Urine Diagnosis	149
18	Medicine, Treatment, Diet and Behavior	154
19	Miscellaneous Treatments	163

1
Introduction

Today at the Kosmos I am meeting all of you who show special interest in Tibetan medicine. And to all of you I extend my greetings and wish that all of us may remain healthy in body and spirit.

To begin with, there are certain conditions to be met by the doctor who gives the medical teachings and by the students who receives the same teachings. There are three particular qualities concerning the doctor who is giving the teachings. First and foremost, the doctor should consider the place where the teaching is being given as a Buddha-field and not just an ordinary place. Secondly, the doctor should not take himself or herself as an ordinary being but, at this particular moment, they should meditate and visualize that he or she is a deity of the Medicine Buddha and is imparting the medical teachings in such a form and spirit. And lastly, the doctor should not condescendingly consider the students as ordinary beings but as gods and goddesses who have come to receive the teachings with a clear and pure mind.

As to the students receiving the teachings, they also have three requisite qualities. Their mental attitude, metaphorically speaking, should not be like a vase which is turned upside-down; or one with a hole in the bottom and lastly they should avoid being like a vase which is filled with the poison of extreme attitudes. In essence, the students should be open, aware and receptive like a flower vase and the teachings of the doctor is the water that is being poured into the open, aware and receptive vase.

In the first example, the vase turned upside-down shows that when the students do not have the openness to receive the medical teachings, then it would be like the doctor trying to pour the water of medical knowledge into a vase that is turned upside-down. Not even a single drop of water will go in.

The second vase that has a hole in the bottom refers to students who do not seriously concentrate or remember the medical teachings. The student merely hears the teachings but forgets them soon afterwards, like the water poured into a vase that has a hole in the bottom. Slowly the water goes out from the hole. Similarly the students slowly forgets the teachings they has merely heard from the doctor.

The third vase which is filled with poison refers to students who have intelligently grasped the teachings properly but who mix and confuse the teachings with the teachings of other traditions and systems, whether it be another system of medicine or of religion or whatever. So whenever he confuses the teachings of one system with another, it becomes perverted and turns into poison. Therefore, whatever medical teachings that one gets, one must keep it clean, pure and true to its tradition. It should not be adulterated.

When one is receiving the medical teachings, the attitude or the intention should be to eventually help and bring benefit to suffering patients. With such a refined and humanitarian attitude, the teachings cannot be polluted and become poisonous. When we are receiving this medical teaching, we should not consider that it is for the use and benefit of this particular life as we might die very soon—no one can be certain about the hour of our death. Receiving a teaching is like planting a seed which creates propensity. If it does not benefit in this particular life, it will surely benefit in the next life. It will be very easy to continue study of the system of medicine or whatever in the next life as the propensity is there from the teachings received in this life.

So, I have explained the qualities and defects concerning the doctor and the medical students.

2

History and Origin of Tibetan Medicine

Before coming to the main topic, let us first briefly discuss the history and origin of Tibetan medicine. The Buddha in his manifestation as the Buddha of Medicine is traditionally regarded as the originator of Tibetan medicine. This Buddha is described as the source of all knowledge pertaining to Tibetan medicine and, though history does not give us enough evidence to prove that he was a doctor of medicine curing physical ailments, there is no reason why we should not regard him as the originator of Tibetan medicine since he cured suffering sentient beings of *samsara* from their spiritual sickness of anger, greed and lust etc.

From recorded history we can glean that during the 5th century when the first Tibetan king Nyatri Tsenpo was ruling Tibet, two great Indian physicians, Vijay and Gajay, came to Tibet from central India. They stayed in Tibet for over a decade imparting their medical knowledge and serving the suffering. In recognition of their service, the Tibetan king is said to have given one of his own queens to Gajay in marriage. To them was born an extraordinary son named Dungi Thorchog, who became an outstanding physician and was appointed as the first physician to the king. Dungi Thorchog's descendants extend to the celebrated family lineage of one of the greatest Tibetan doctors of all time, the now-famous Yuthok Yonten Gonpo Sarma of 18th century Tibet. The emigration of Gajay and Vijay from central India to Tibet and birth and accomplishment of Dungyi Thorchog is regarded as the dawn of Tibetan medicine. However, recent research has revealed that quite an advanced system of Tibetan medicine and astrology like divination, sortilege, etc. of Shangshung, was in existence in Tibet itself when the dominant social philosophy and religion was not Buddhism but Bon. Because Buddhism became the state religion later, it seems the Bon heritage and its rich medicine and astrology suffered a partial eclipse.

The second chapter of Tibetan medicine begins with the emergence of Lodroe Sinyen during the later part of the reign of the famous Tibetan king Songtsen Gampo (Srong-bTsan sGam-po—629-649). Lodroe Sinyen historically belonged to the same ancestry as Dun-gyi Thorchog. As the transmission of medical knowledge was strictly oral between the hereditary teacher and student, Lodroe Sinyen is said to have introduced the recording of medical writings in Tibet. His son Yuthok Drechi Becha was equally famous and visited India three times. In his time the Four Medical Tantras which forms the root text of Tibetan medicine were translated into Tibetan from Sanskrit. His son Yuthok Khyongpo fathered Yuthok Yonten Gonpo, an extraordinary and brilliant doctor in the history of Tibetan medicine. Under his personal initiative and supervision, a number of very important medical treatises, texts and other related writings were compiled for the first time. Like his grandfather Yuthok Drechi Becha, he visited India three times to research and compare the Tibetan and Indian Ayurvedic systems of medicine. He lived to the ripe old age of 125 years and produced medical treatises like *Cha-lag Cho-gye* (Cha-lag bCho-rgyas), *De-khor Cho-gye* (sDe-'khor bCho-rgyas) and *Shog-dril Kor-sum* (Shog-bsGril Skor-gsum), the second of which is a text on surgery.

The first international debate on Tibetan medicine took place during the reign of King Trisong Deutsen (Khri-srong lde'u-btsan—755-97) when skilled doctors from Mongolia, China, India, Persia, Eastern Turkistan, Nepal, Kashmir, Dolpo, Afghanistan and so on participated. The debate took place at Samye in Lhasa. The Tibetan delegation was led by Yuthok Yonten Gonpo Nyingma. The conference lasted for several days, with each doctor expounded the nature and efficacy of his own system.

After the conference King Trisong Deutsen promulgated a code of behavior to be observed by all the physicians. Known as The Four Vows, it specified that a doctor must be altruistic, abandon sloth and procrastination, abstain from intoxicating drinks and most importantly make a patient at ease and relieved through compassion and love.

One of the descendant of Yuthok Yonten Gonpo Nyingma known as Yuthok Yonten Gonpo Sarma lived in 18th century Tibet and is credited with the authorship of a new version of the *Four Medical Tantras*. It is believed that he travelled to Persia when only eighteen years old to study medicine and authored the most exhaustive commentary on the *Four Medical Tantras* entitled *The Eighteen Auxiliary Aids*. The periods covered by the two Yuthok Yonten Gonpos can be considered the golden age of Tibetan medicine. Later the study and research of Tibetan medicine received special attention under the patronage of the Great Fifth Dalai Lama, whose regent Sangye Gyatso (Sangs-rgyas rGya-mTsho) was a very brilliant medical and astrological scholar. The first Tibetan medical college was founded by him at Chakpori hill in Lhasa in 1950. In 1916, the Tibetan Astro-Medical Center or Men-tsi khang (sMan-rTsis Khang) was founded by Khyenrab Norbu (mKhyen-rab Nor-bu) under the patronage of the Great Thirteenth Dalai Lama. This is a brief history of the origin and development of Tibetan medicine. However, it was not only in Lhasa that medicine and astrology flourished. Elsewhere in Tibet, in the provinces like Kham, Amdo, Tsang and Tod, medicine and astrology were diligently taught and studied. Such pockets of medical and astrological learning produced their own astrologers and physicians. I also belong to one such tributary of medical and astrological learning that had its roots in Kyirong (sKyid-grong) in western Tibet. I obtained my medical and astrological teachings from my root Guru Palbar Gen Rinpoche and I was trained in the practice of the medical art by my father Dr. Tsering Wangdu Khangkar. Once in exile, after the devastating Chinese invasion, the hard conditions of material and spiritual life forced me to abandon the practice of medicine for some time. I donated many of my medical manuscripts, etc. to Dharamsala where the center of medicine and astrology was being re-organized. Fortunately, with the profound blessings and profuse inspiration of the immaculate wisdom of Kyabje Trijang Dorjee Chang, the junior tutor of His Holiness the Dalai Lama, I was spiritually and materially guided and encouraged to take up my hereditary profession of medicine once again. It was Kyabje Trijang Rinpoche who advised me to join the newly founded Tibetan Medical Center. When I applied for admission, the administrators at that time told me that in the whole history of Men-tsi Khang, there was no records of a woman doctor and instead sent me to Dalhousie Tibetan School as a foster mother. On the advice of Kyabje Rinpoche, the principal of the school, Samdong Rinpoche, allowed me to practice my ancestral profession of medicine in the school. Starting from a small clinic in Dalhousie in the mid-sixties, I have ceaselessly practiced medicine, not forgetting to train my daughters in the tradition, and always prayed to my spiritual protectors to enable me to serve the suffering patients of any and every nationality with the medical knowledge and experience that I am bestowed with. Like me, there are numerous doctors in every part of Tibet that have their hereditary knowledge and individual gifts and talent to contribute towards the growth and progress of Tibetan medicine.

3

The Four Tantras

Yuthok Yonten Gonpo the Younger revised all the medical teachings that were in existence in Tibet. He took what was right and pure and discarded what was not pertinent or relevant. Based on this eclectic compilation from the medical knowledge that existed, he compiled and created the Four Medical Tantras. Each of the four tantras have sections or chapters which are particular to these tantras. They differ. Each of them do not have exactly the same divisions.

The Root Tantra, which is the first one, has six sections. In this first—the root tantra—everything is exemplified as a tree with its roots, trunk and branches. All the sicknesses and their characteristics are drawn into the tree.

We will just give an example now as it will take a very long time to study this tree in full, I will give an example just to make an impression. The trunk of the tree has one root. From that single root comes three branches. Each of the three branches sprout out a leaf. What is this leaf? This indicates the causes of disease. There are two kinds of causes. One is a distant cause and the other is an immediate cause.

What is the distant cause of a disease? The distant cause is that from our birth we have *ma rig-pa*—which is a basic ignorance of not being able to understand one's own basic nature. Out of this ignorance—of not being able to know what is what—springs the three emotions of passion, aggression and stupidity or dullness. These three constitute the distant cause.

I will explain this through an example: when an eagle, for instance, is flying in the sky, its body casts a shadow on the earth. Because it is flying very high in the sky, it does not see its shadow. It does not mean that the shadow does not exist. It only means that the eagle does not see the shadow, but the shadow is always there. This is basic ignorance.

So now we will consider the immediate cause. The immediate cause of our diseases are wind or vital current, bile or vital energy, and phlegm or vital arabolic force. In Tibetan they are known as lung (*rlung*: Vital energy), tripa (*mkhris-pa*: bile) and *Bad-kan* (phlegm).

There is a legend concerning the origin of the rlung disease. In the Tibetan medical tradition, it is mentioned that there was a goddess who lived in the sea. Her commitment was to keep a ballon of rlung or wind under her armpit. Once she arose out of the sea and saw a man with whom she became infatuated. So they had sexual intercourse and in the process the goddess forgot about holding the rLung under her armpit. She was committed never to let the rLung to spread among all the sentient beings and her lapse is how the diseases connected with rlung came about.

Actually, *rlung* is not something new. It has been with us from the time of our conception in the mother's womb. It is the vehicle for the fine consciousness, the seed of subtle consciousness. To form the human body, there are five different kinds of *rlung*. If these five act in the negative way they cause imbalance in the humors which cause disease. If they act in a positive way, the balance is maintained and there is harmony in the body.

Now let us discuss *mkhris-pa* or bile. It arises in connection with the emotion of anger or aggression. When there is aggression, when one feels angry, then there is a connection with the heart and the liver. The result of this alteration caused by anger is that the level of blood increases, and there is an increase in the level of blood coming from the liver into the heart. Then the *mkhris-pa* is increased. So the immediate cause would be anger. Anger produce more bile. And all the diseases connected with bile are connected with this cause.

The legend of how *mkhris-pa* or bile originated in the beginning must be told. This is actually something that we in our tradition believe happened. In ancient India there was a Brahmin who served the holy beings who depended on alms for their subsistence. The daughter of the Brahmin one day invited both Lord Buddha and Lord Shiva to attend a congregation in their house. Lord Shiva came a bit late and could not find a seat. So he stayed at the back. When the food was served, Lord Shiva was served last as he was in the back. Taking offence at this, Lord Shiva emitted a fire from his forehead intending to burn the congregation. Since the congregation consisted of Lord Buddha and his disciples, the fire could not burn them and instead spread to the world originating the *mkhris-pa* or bile disease.

Let us now talk about *Bad-kan* or phlegm. It arises from the emotion of dullness and stupidity. In Tibetan this emotion is called *gto-mug*. *Bad-kan*, supported by the brain, is located in the upper region of the body.

To enumerate the legend concerning the origin of *Bad-kan*, it is written that in ancient time in India, a king had a minister whose head was that of a horse. Unfortunately for the king, his queen fell in love with the minister and secretly stayed with him. On learning this, the king became angry and put both the minister and the queen in the box and threw them into the river. The dying queen and the minister made a curse that the king should die from the diseases of *bad-kan*. He lost the warmth in his stomach and could not properly digest food. He also had diarrhoea. Now the king was very angry. At that time, the mythical bird known as the *garuda* came to the king. The angry king threw his own excrement on the bird who flew all over the world and cleaned off the king's feces on its way. So this stench and dirt fell on the sentient beings and the disease of *bad-kan* originated. When we mention that the nature of *bad-kan* is water, this is the reason.

This is the first leaf of the tree that we are considering.

Now we will consider the middle leaf concerning the seven physical constituents of the body and the three excretory matters. The seven physical constituents are:

nutritional essence
blood
muscle tissue
adipose tissue
bone tissue
bone marrow
sperm or ovum

The three excretory matters are:

feces
urine
sweat

The third leaf we are considering is related with the five sense organs. The five sense organs are:

sight
hearing
smelling
taste
touch

After organizing the medical tree and its three important leaves, we can get into a discussion of the science of medicine itself, including the different treatments explained in the six different branches of this specific tantra. In this way, we will cover all the six divisions of the first tantra.

Next comes the second tantra known as the *Explanatory Tantra* which consists of 32 divisions. For instances, there is a section considering the conception of child in the womb, another section discusses how disease manifests, comes about and increases. Still another section specifies the conditions of circumstances that brings about a disease.

Some chapters talk about diagnosis of the pulse, diagnosis of urine, etc., while other chapters talk about treatment like moxa, acupuncture, blood-letting, etc.

The fourth tantra is called *The Secret Tantra* or *The Tantra of Oral Instruction*. For this fourth tantra to be taught by a doctor, the right students should be there—students who are the perfect vases to receive the secret water of the medical knowledge contained in this tantra. They are not given to anyone just like that. Most disciples or students do not have the right qualifications to receive this medical teaching. That is why the fourth tantra is called the Secret Oral Tantra. The student who is merely curious about Tibetan medicine will not be taught this tantra. We will just briefly discuss the two sections of this tantra.

When a Tibetan doctor is applying moxa, he or she will take the right measurements of the body of the patient to specify and localize the right point where the moxa will be applied. Before lighting the spark of the moxa, the doctor will imagine or visualize himself or herself as a god or goddess and invite the eight manifestations of the Buddha of Medicine and the deities and protectors of his or her own lineage. After offering prayers of prostrations and obeisance to the Buddha of Medicine and the deities, the doctor should imagine that the burning of the moxa will produce aromatic scent that is beneficial to the patient and that the fire will act as a fierce enemy to frighten away the disease and other harmful and negative influence connected with that disease. Actually, during the moxa treatment there will be some bad smell because of the burning, which can irritate and anger certain kinds of spirits or beings that are considered sacred in the tradition. Therefore, the doctor should explain to these spirits, tell them through the chanting of mantras that the bad smell is not to disturb them. One's own body has a collection of deities. They should also be prayed to and told that the smell is not intended to harm them. After these preparations, the moxa is applied.

If the doctor wants to cure a cold disease like *bad-kan* by applying moxa, the application of this treatment would help in increasing the warmth of the body. In the case of a hot problem like fever which affects the intestine, stomach and other digestive systems, turning the fat in the body of a patient into ulcer, or if there are problems in digestion causing diarrhoea, the application of moxa can prevent such problems.

When a patient is suffering from a disease of the *rlung* or wind penetrating through all the orifices of the body, it will be useful to stop the wind or vital currents from escaping. With the application of moxa, the pathways of the wind will be blocked and the *rlung* kept without increasing any further. Also by applying moxa, any part of the body that has an infection can be cured as the moxa will dry up the pus. The application of moxa can cast away the conditions or circumstances which lead to sickness and prevent the harmful influence of negative forces and so forth.

It is important for a doctor to visualize himself or herself as a deity while applying the moxa as it will have a favorable influence. When a doctor does not visualize himself or herself as a deity but just acts in an ordinary way and applies the moxa for a particular disease on a specific point—carrying out the technique properly but without the benefit of visualizing himself or herself as a deity—then the doctor will be able to cure only that particular disease and fail to influence the 424 types of diseases which a moxa application, from a doctor who has the spiritual standard to visualize oneself as a deity, can influence.

There is a special time and day for the application of moxa. One can not apply moxa treatment on Tuesdays, Saturdays, and Sundays. These are negative days to apply moxa. Why is this so? For instance, Tuesday is of the nature of fire. The element of fire is predominant; if one applies moxa which is also fire, then the treatment will have very bad effect.

There are specified days of the month when moxa can be applied. These days are recognized and established according to the movement of a certain deity in our body. The deity—a goddess—keeps going around our body all the time. So on the specified days one can be certain the goddess will be at a particular point in the body. For example, on a certain day at a certain hour the goddess is in the shoulder and one applies moxa on that very point in the shoulder, the goddess will be harmed and this will result in the shortening of the life of the patient. Therefore, a doctor who applies moxa must know the favorable and unfavorable days and hours of applying this treatment.

From the first to the tenth day of the Tibetan month, the doctor should not apply moxa to the upper part of the body starting from the heart to the head. From the tenth to the twentieth day, the doctor should not apply moxa in that part of the body from the heart going down to the kidneys. From the twentieth to the thirtieth day of the Tibetan month, the doctor should not apply moxa from the lower part of the kidneys all the way down to the feet. The doctor should not apply moxa on the full moon. Why is this so? This is because the goddess in the body is going all over the body. Also on the last day of the Tibetan month when there is no moon, moxa should not be applied as the moxa will conflict with the body.

This strict reference to a specific time of moxa treatment is very important because the treatment, instead of benefitting a patient, might result in creating more problems for the patient. For instance, when a doctor is applying moxa or is doing bloodletting or surgery, if he or she fails to take note of the proper and favorable timing, the patient will be in danger and suffer the consequences.

Now we have talked very briefly about the Four Tantras and their contents.

4
The Training of the Tibetan Doctor

We will talk now, also very briefly, about the training of the Tibetan doctor.

A student who is going to be trained as a doctor, before the actual medical training, should be able to read proficiently and be able to separate the words from each other and comprehend the whole construction of the sentences so that the student may not be confused in reading the texts.

After becoming proficient in reading, the student will start learning spelling and calligraphy. This is very important in learning Tibetan language as mistakes in spelling will change the meaning of the sentence.

When the student has mastered reading, writing and spelling, he or she must study the synonyms as each Tibetan medicine or its ingredients have four, five, six or seven or more names. The actual medicine or the ingredient is one. However, there are different ways of calling it. Therefore the student must study the synonyms.

After a complete study of the synonyms, the student must pursue the mastery of the grammar of Tibetan language, which is very important. After grammar comes verse writing or the study of poetry. The student, after some years of studying grammar and poetry, must be in a position to compose poetry independently and also compose an essay which he or she must submit to the teacher, who will examine it. If he is able to secure 80 or 90 percent in this, the student will be judged qualified for further training.

After completing this basic training, the student can choose a subject of his or her liking. They can either pursue Thangka painting, medicine, astrology or any other subject that has captivated their interest. If the student decides to study medicine, then his or her training as a doctor will begin.

The student now entering the school of medicine must have perseverance in the tasks ahead. He or she should not tire easily from chores like going up to the mountains to choose and collect medicinal herbs. The student must be energetic and think of facing any hardship connected with the medical training he or she is undergoing with enthusiasm.

The student now must memorize the medical verses which condenses the essential meanings of the *Four Tantras*. The teacher will examine by making the student recite the book of medical verses from memory. Simultaneously, the teacher gives instructions to the students on the different herbal ingredients of medicine and will personally take them to the different regions where these herbs are grown, in the correct seasons. The doctor or the teacher will show the students how to recognize the right herbs and how to pluck and collect the right parts of the herbs whether it is a flower, leaf or a root that is required of a particular ingredient. To test the students, the doctor will gather similar kinds of medicinal herbs that taste alike, look alike and smell alike so that the students are able to differentiate the right from the wrong and select the correct one.

There is a series of examinations that the students have to undergo in their medical training. The first one takes place after one year. The examination is both written and oral. For instance, the teacher would ask the student to write about the seven constituents of the body and the student must write it down and show it to the teacher. Similarly, the teacher will ask the student to recite from memory a chapter from the medical text and the student must be able to recite it without any lapse.

The training of the medical student will usually last for seven years. Each year there will be a new focus of study and training. During the first three years, the student will remain close to the teacher and will acquire knowledge from the experience of the teacher. During the seven years of preliminary training is when the student will memorize medical texts, recognize and collect medicinal herbs and be introduced to examining the urine and general pulse of the patient, etc. After these seven years of intensive basic training, the student will stay close to the teacher and learn the more complicated aspects of pulse diagnosis. The first step for the student is to detect the natural or constant pulse of the patient. Once the student is able to detect the different kinds of pulses—male, female and neutral—the teacher will explain the procedure of examining and recognizing the pulses indicating disturbances in the rLung, mKhris-pa and Bad-kan. During the training of pulse diagnosis, the student will be asked to check patients and record the diagnosis. From this record the teacher will assess the performance of the students. This is an examination of the experience gained by the students. After the pulse diagnosis training, the students will also be taught the different types of treatment and therapies like moxabustion, blood-letting, acupuncture, midwifery, massage, etc. The student will also gain experience in treating insanity and paranoia. The person who is insane is treated in a medical and psychological way. The teacher will teach the student how to talk sweetly and comfortingly to such a patient, taking into consideration the special characteristics of the insanity.

After completing ten full years of study and training in Tibetan medical sciences, the student will be made to examine about a hundred patients daily. The record of the diagnosis will be kept. In this graduation examination, the student will be on his or her own and, by only be examining the pulse, must come to right diagnosis and determine the sickness of the patient. If the student is able to read correctly 80 cases out of one hundred, he or she will be considered fit for medical practice. If the percentage is lower than that, the student may be asked to spend a further year of practical study and training with the teacher.

Once the medical student graduates and leaves the medical school, he or she is on her own. What the student has studied in the institute becomes like a weapon with which he or she must fight the sickness of the suffering patients. In a sense, his or her real education and training then begins—when on their own they must diagnose and prescribe medicines and await the result of their treatment.

This is a brief description of the training of a Tibetan doctor.

5
The Three Humors

This morning we have completed an account of the training of a Tibetan doctor. Now I would like to talk about the three humors called *rlung*, *mkhris-pa* and *bad-kan*, loosely translated as wind, bile and phlegm. These three can be of harm and also they can be of benefit. So, we will talk about their qualities as well as the problems they are capable of producing. In the classical Tibetan medical treatise entitled *The Secret Oral Instructions on the Eight Branches of the Science of Tibetan Medicine* it is written: "There are three classifications of humors, bodily constituents and impurities. Their balance and imbalance cause the body to thrive or to over come. The humors are *rlung*, *mkhri-pa* and *bad-kan*."

rLung

rLung is not something new. It has been with us from the time of our conception in the mother's womb. It is the vehicle of the fine consciousness, the seed of subtle consciousness. According to Tibetan medical theory, *rlung* serves as the medium for consciousness, enabling it to move from one object to another just as a horse serves as a mount for a rider to journey from one place to another. Furthermore, the human mind possess the light fluctuating nature of *rlung*, and human consciousness itself is dependent on the *rlung* energy to successfully and clearly ascertain its awareness of subject and object. Physically, *rlung* serves as the basis for skeletal muscle, nerve, vascular, hormonal and membrane transport activity. On a more subtle end, *rlung* serves as the basis for mental and sense consciousness, linking the mind inseparably to the body. As such, *rlung* is also of the mind but not the mind itself. A disturbance in the *rlung* causes mental disorders. In everyday Tibetan language, *rlung* is associated with the anger of the mind causing violent mental and emotional derangement.

To form the human body, there are five different kinds of rLung. If these five *rlung* act in a negative way, they cause disease due to imbalance. If these five *rlung* act in a positive way, then our body remains in balance, and the body remains healthy.

Now I will explain each *rlung* and how it acts in our body.

1. Srog-zin rlung:
This can be roughly translated as life-sustaining energy. This *rlung* or energy is located at the heart and also at the crown of the head. Its movement is between head and chest. This energy gives such vital energy to the heart that it enables the person to perform any work with pride and without any fear. It enables swallowing, spitting, sneezing and respiration. It also provides clarity to one's mind and the sensory organs. This *rlung* can be further sub-divided into five secondary *rlung*, each serving as the basis for the five sense consciousnesses of sight, hearing, smell, taste and touch. If this *rlung* works in a negative way, it causes mental disorders, nervousness and the weariness making a person feel sad without any cause.

2. Geng-du rlung:
This can be translated as an ascending vital energy. This is located in the chest, but circulates through the nose, tongue and throat

regions. This *rlung* provides the human body with speech power, breathing power, sputum or saliva, and the ability to spit and swallow. If this *rlung* does not function properly it causes problems in the throat, causing congestion and blockage which is often mistaken as sore throat. If it is not properly diagnosed and treated at the beginning, patients are then fed through a pipe, causing numerous difficulties. It should be accurately diagnosed as a *rlung* problem caused by the ascending *rlung* located in the chest which can be treated.

3. Kyab-che rlung:
It can be translated as the all-pervasive or diffusive vital energy which is located variously at the heart or crown of the head. It also pervades from the brain to the toes of the foot, especially in the joints. It helps in the extension of the limbs, muscular action, physical growth and smooth performance of the bodily functions in perceiving or identifying objects. A disorder in this rLung can cause weak eyesight and poor memory.

4. Me-nyam rlung:
It can be translated as fire-accompanying or metabolic energy. This energy is located in the stomach and the digestive systems. It also circulates in all the hollow parts of the body including the nerves and the blood vessels. It works on all the foods, solids or liquids, helping the overall digestive system by taking out the essence of any good substance and thus giving strength and energy to the whole body. In short, it purifies the digestive system. If this rLung works in a negative way, it causes liver weakness, gastric trouble, nausea, constipation, etc.

5. Thur-sel rlung:
Translated as descending energy, it is located in the pelvic regions. Circulating through the gastrointestinal tract, large intestine and the genitals, this *rlung* controls the flow of urine, semen, ovulation and excretion as well as menstruation and childbirth.

This concludes a brief explanation of *rlung* according to Tibetan medicine.

Q. These energies are formed at contact with the mother and these control bodily functions after contact with mother. Where does energy to control come from before contact with mother?

A. Even when we die, the fine consciousness never dies.

Q. Sorry, I misunderstood. What you meant by contact with mother, is this conception or after birth?

A. Before contact with mother there is a fine consciousness which becomes the heart after contact. Then before the other four *rlung* develop there is one energy, fine consciousness, located in the heart. This always remains, whether we die or not.

Q. Do you call that *son tsing* or a different name?

A. When it is strong energy it is called *tson tsing rlung*. When it has little power of energy it is called *meshi tson tigle*. Translated directly it means "everlasting life-consciousness." Everlasting life. In Christian terms it means "the soul never dies." You should understand the meaning even after we pass away, this consciousness never dies. Everlasting. An easy way to explain this is as follows: any machine, a car, must have air pushing the petrol, so we also do not work without energy. If rLung is not there, it is like losing a very main organ. We do not know what you call it in Western medical terminology but we call it *rlung*.

Q. Which rLung controls fetal development?

A. There is a fine consciousness before the child's contact with the mother. After contact is made, *rlung* is produced in the veins or nerves. Once contact is made in the womb, 38 different *rlung*, one each week, are produced in the veins to form the complete baby. If there is early delivery then perhaps the baby hasn't developed complete *rlung* energy. So an early delivery baby may have speech problems, nervousness and shivering, for the child does not have the full energy of *rlung*. This causes the symptoms of disease.

Q. What *rlung* controls the uterus in woman and testes in man? How does the *rlung* lead to control this?

A. *Thur-sel rlung* acts in two ways, passing and controlling. When it is overactive, it cannot pass. If less active, it cannot control. It controls all urinary functions as well.

Q. If the mother has an imbalance of *rlung* energies does this affect the child? Does it harm the child?
A. This doesn't affect the child, but if the mother has a sore or ulcer in the womb, it could. A baby has its own *rlung* system.

Q. Where is *thur-sel rlung* located?
A. It is located at the anus, or rather in the anus, the holding shape on the 4th line. If *thur-sel rlung* is not working properly, it causes different diseases, like bile and haemoroids.

Q. Can *thur-sel rlung* cause a person to be sterile?
A. If the female has something wrong with the *thur-sel rlung* then she cannot conceive babies. The *rlung* cannot draw in the semen of the man. After menstruation, the womb is open for 12 days. During these 12 days, if the *thur-sel rlung* has no energy it cannot draw the semen in. After 12 days, there is no contact between the male sperm and the female egg.

Q. If one *rlung* is working in the wrong way, will the rest be alright? If one is wrong will all the rest be wrong?
A. No, because of different locations. If one *rlung* is wrong, the other *rlung* will be normal. *rlung* is a general name. For example, suppose out of Sydney, Canberra and Melbourne, it is raining at Sydney, it does not effect Canberra or Melbourne.

Q. So there is no connection between all the *rlung*?
A. Yes there are connections between them. *Srog-zin rlung* is connected with *geng-du rlung*, *thur-sel rlung* with *me-nyam* and *srog-zin* with *kyab-che rlung* and so forth. If *srog-zin* and *kyab-che rlung* are not working properly, then the patient becomes crazy.

Q. Are the five *rlung*s connected with the chakras?
A. The nature of the chakra is *rlung*. So there is a connection. Each chakra is separated by eight finger widths.

Q. There are yoga exercises to open chakras. Do they effect *rlung*?
A. If you do yoga with too much concentration, then you cannot cause the *rlung* to block. Or if you squeeze your body too much or it is pressed too much then this can cause the *rlung* to not circulate properly. Suppose you are walking very fast and mentally your mind is racing, then you get *rlung* problems. This will cause nervousness, depression and so on.

Q. What gives energy to the *rlung*?
A. *rLung* itself has its own energy. Its nature is energy. So it is not dependent on other energies.

Q. Can you increase your *rlung*? Can you make them stronger?
A. Yes.

Q. How can you change *rlung*?
A. There are three ways: diet, medicine and behavior. With diet, food should be cooked, not eaten raw or cold. Also swimming is good, and breathing exercises in high mountains. For example, in this room there is no air, nor windows, so we cannot get enough *rlung* energy. Our eyes feel tired, we feel lazy, this means that *rlung* energy is decreasing. So what we have been talking about is just *rlung*. There are also two other energies that work with *rlung* to form the body and help it to function well. They are bile and phlegm. *rLung* is general name there are five different *rlung*s on which I already spoke.

Q. Before the birth, in the fine consciousness, is there any prior individuality that connects mother to child?
A. There is no individuality. The contact is due to karma. Fine consciousness is like a seed. It is cultivated in the field and then it grows. This seed grows leaves and fruit, and so it is in forming the mind. So as this fine consciousness is the seed, we all grow up as human forms but we do not have the same face or exactly same shape. This is due to karma, past actions. Therefore we do good things in this life, so that when the seed is fertilized in the next life, it will grow well. So this life is very important. We should cultivate this life.

Q. When you feel the pulse, do you feel the *rlung*?
A. Yes, you can feel *rlung*, bile and phlegm individually because in diagnosis they are located as different pulses. Bile has a hot quality, phlegm has a cool quality. *rLung* and phlegm are cold, and bile is hot. *rLung* is more powerful than phlegm or bile, because *rlung* makes contact with bile and phlegm and goes to both. So *rlung* causes the disease. Suppose we blow a fire, then we cause more heat to arise. The nature of the bile is hot so if *rlung* comes then bile produces more heat. Bile is only a name. By using the name we understand the quality. Each of the three have their own qualities. They have their own different way of acting. Their way of acting is different and separate, but they act together in their different ways in our body to keep it healthy and strong. The location of the bile is below the liver. In the liver, blood is purified. Good pure blood goes back to our body, the second becomes bile. Bile and blood are both heat in nature.

Q. Where is blood made?
A. The first production of blood is from the parents. The father's semen produces the brain and all the bones. From the mother comes blood, flesh and skin. So at the point of contact between the father and the mother, and from the fine consciousness of the child, all inner organs are produced and act in different ways.

Q. Is there any place in the body where blood is made?
A. In the liver and spleen. When there is hepatitis and jaundice, the spleen and liver are not producing blood. In the Tibetan system, blood is mainly produced by the liver. If a kidney were removed the person can still live but if the liver is taken out, then that person will not live. It is a main organ. In the Tibetan medical text, the heart is the king, the liver is the queen, the lungs are ministers and the organs, large intestines and small intestines, kidneys, etc. are the public or staff members. So losing one of the staff makes little difference.

mKhris-pa

So now we will consider bile or *mkhris-pa*. It is also of five different types residing in five different locations. The first type of bile is known as *mkhris-pa 'ju-byed* which primarily means a bile that helps digestion and separation of the essential nutrients from the miscellaneous foodstuffs ingested. This digestive bile or *'ju-byed* is situated between the stomach and the intestines. Besides helping with digestion and separation of the essential nutrients, *mkhris-pa 'ju-byed* also helps in stimulating bodily heat and provides numerous facilities to assist in the proper and balanced functioning of the remaining four *mkhris-pa* energies.

The second bile is known as *mkhris-pa sgrub-byed* or accomplishing bile. This bile is situated in the chest and heart region and partly governs our conduct of good and bad actions. It is responsible for the mind's initial thoughts of pride, ambition, desire, etc. Its symptoms of disorder are unclear memory and awareness and the need for too much sleep.

The third type of bile is known as *mkhris-pa mthong-byed* which can be translated as visually operating bile. This bile resides in the eyes and is responsible for vision and clarity. The symptoms of such a bile disorder are inability to gaze at the sun and seeing white objects as yellow.

The fourth bile is known as *mkhris-pa mdangs-sgyur* or color transforming bile. It resides in the liver and is mainly responsible for haemoglobin or the red coloring of blood and muscle tissues. Its symptoms of disorder are itching and yellowing of the skin.

The fifth bile is known as *mdog-gsal mkhris-pa* or the complexion clearing bile. Residing in the skin, it is responsible for the color of the skin. As a symptom of its disorder, the skin turns rough and dark blue, the hairs of the head and the eyebrows wither or fall. The fingernails turn dark and the body becomes weak.

This completes a brief explanation of the five different types of bile or *mkhris-pa*.

Bad-kan

Now we will discuss about *bad-kan* or phlegm. The humor *bad-kan* is also of five types. The first *bad-kan* known as *rten-byed* or supportive phlegm is located around the thoracic and abdominal region. Its main function is to regulate bodily fluids and support the remaining four *bad-kan*. Symptoms of disorders of this *bad-kan* include loss or lack of appetite, frequent vomiting of sour fluid, shooting pains in the upper trunk and also a feeling of heat in the breast-bone.

The second type of phlegm known as *bad-kan myad-byed* or mixing phlegm resides in the epigastric region. Its main function is to break the solid foodstuffs into a semi-liquid state and mix them for proper digestion. Symptoms of a disorder in this phlegm would be poor digestion, tightness of the abdomen accompanied by frequent belching and vomiting of any food as soon as it is consumed.

The third type of phlegm is known as *bad-kan myong-byed* or experiencing phlegm. This resides in the tongue and is responsible for the six tastes of sweet, sour, salty, bitter, astringent and acrid. Symptoms of a disorder in this phlegm would be inability to distinguish tastes, lack of thirst, a cold feeling in the tongue, roughness of the voice and an up-turn in the upper lip and a down-turn in the lower lip.

The fourth phlegm is known as *bad-kan tsim-byed* or satisfying phlegm. This is located in the head and is responsible for the satisfaction of the five senses. Symptoms of a disorder with this phlegm are visual distortion, frequent sneezing, a feeling of heaviness on one side of the head and frequent influenza.

The fifth phlegm known as *bad-kan 'byor-byed* means connecting phlegm. This phlegm resides in the joints and is responsible for the articulations of the body e.g. flexion, abduction, circulation, adduction, etc. Symptoms of a disorder in this phlegm are difficulty in extending and retracting the limbs, thickness of the joints, a loose feeling and pain in the shoulders and hip joints, plus swelling of all the joints.

This completes a brief explanation of the five types of *bad-kan* or phlegm.

6
The Functions of the Three Humors

We have now completed a discussion of the 15 subdivisions of humors that exist in the human body. Now we will talk about each of them in terms of their function, in terms of their ability.

We will start with the first *rlung* known as *srog-zin*, the life sustaining energy. This is located in the crown of one's head. Which are the pathways this energy takes in order to circulate in the body? In the head there are three pathways in which this energy moves and circulates. Next it circulates from the neck to this depression that exists in the chest. From the inner throat it moves down to the chest. The function of this energy is to help in swallowing food and assisting in the movement of the tongue when we are drinking. Both such actions are controlled by this life-sustaining energy. When one eats food, then one breathes. This breathing is also controlled by this energy. Also it is responsible for being able to swallow saliva and to spit. When we have dirt in the nose, we have to clean it by blowing the nose. This energy is also responsible for that ability to blow the nose.

We will examine the second one which resides in the chest and is called *geng-du rlung* or the ascending vital energy. The pathways or the channels where this energy moves are the nose, the tongue and the area inside right beneath the chin. This energy has many functions which develop in this side of the body. It has many kinds of functions and abilities. The first function is that one is the ability to emit sounds, whether subtle or loud, whether long or short. This ability to emit a specific sound is the result of this energy. Then within the body itself, this energy is responsible for the other four vital energies or rLung, to develop strength in the body, etc. This energy is also responsible for the different colors that one has in the body. For instance, in our eyes, sometimes there are some reddish and some whitish colors. This energy is responsible for making them uniform.

This energy is also responsible for exertion, the ability to make effort. This energy which is responsible for strengthening the body. It is also responsible for a clear memory. If this ascending vital energy works properly, one is able to remember things or events very precisely. One is able to remember things from way back in the past, such as when one was just a child.

Now we will examine the third *rlung* known as *kyab-che* or the all pervasive or diffusive vital energy. It resides mainly in the heart. The heart has many veins but we will mainly consider five veins that are the most important. These five main veins are the central vein surrounded by the other four: one to the left, one to right, one to the front and one at the back. The central vein is the residence of the consciousness and whatever mental activity is done always refers to this main vein, this central vein. There is a pathway that can be seen when the heart is open. This is central vein. It is also a vein where the central channel is located. At the time of conception, and when the embryo begins to grow, this is the first vein to be produced. It is in the actual heart of the person. The heart is composed of flesh and of many kinds of veins, small veins and big veins. Then in the center of the heart there are these five veins. If we look at it from the point of view of Buddhist philosophy, then this is the office or the channel where the mind moves. This central channel or vein is in the heart, which is also called the entrance of the mind. When this entrance of the mind is blocked, the mind has bad dreams, sees bad omens or is unhappy. Also there is a point of the vein, which is pointing either to the left or to the right. It is because of this point that a Tibetan doctor will examine females from the right arm and the males from the left arm. Depending on the direction towards which this vein is pointing also determines a male with more courage than a woman and a woman with the inclination to become afraid more quickly than a man.

This energy is referred to as all pervasive or diffusive simply because it has the ability to completely penetrate or pervade throughout the body, from the top of the head to the tip of the toes. The heart can spread the blood throughout the whole body, and this energy is responsible for this activity of the heart. This energy is also responsible for the ability to lift the legs, to walk, to bend, and so forth. The movement of the eyes and the mouth, like being able to open the mouth very quickly, to smile and to blink the eyes, all these actions are controlled by this pervasive vital energy.

Now we will consider the *me-nyam rlung* or the fire accompanying vital energy. This resides in the stomach. Not only does it circulate in the intestines, it also moves inside the whole of stomach. Whenever we eat any kind of food, whether raw or cooked, and whenever we drink sweet or sour drinks, the ability of the stomach to digest depends on this rLung. After everything is digested, this energy is responsible for separating the nutrients of this food from the residue and sending and spreading the blood nutrients to all the organs in the body. For example, if there is not good digestion, then the nutrients can not be extracted from the food and the blood will not feed the liver to gain strength. Therefore this energy must work to ripen the blood required in the body.

Now the last *rlung* is *thur-sel* or descending energy. This is located in the pelvic regions. It ciruculates through the large intestines into the colon and finally through the anus. So it is responsible for clearing all that kind of excrement. It also circulates in the urinary bladder. And for women, it is also responsible for cleansing the uterus of menstrual blood and discharging the menstrual blood. In the case of a woman, when this energy malfunctions, she will have problems with irregular periods, meaning the menstruation does not come at the right time, and when it comes it may be a bit solid and not in the right consistency. Also at the time of delivery, when the child is coming out, the mother has no strength to push the child out. This is also a result of malfunction in this energy. In general, for both men and women, this energy is responsible for being able to defecate and urinate.

Q. When you were talking about a malfunction of bile, in which the person would see a white conchshell as yellowish, did you mean that he would be like color-blind or did you mean that the person himself would be yellowish?
A. Because the bile that controls perfection of seeing is not functioning properly, the person with jaundice would actually see everything as yellow. He would look at the moon and see it as yellow, not as white and so forth. The person himself would not be yellow in color, only the perception.

Q. What of color-blindness when a person mixes up blue with green?
A. Blue is connected with *rlung* and the green color is connected with the organ of the spleen. So when a person confuses these two colors, it is because he or she has a malfunction of these two, the workings of the *rlung* and the spleen.

Q. What is the connection between the repeating of mantras and the *rlung*?
A. If a person has complete control over their *rlung*, the chanting of mantras is very important. Based on the control that a person has

on the *rlung*, the reciting of mantra could be very powerful. Based on that power, their meditation will be very powerful. The person can, based on this command that he or she has on the *rlung*, transform the body into the vajra body and achieve a kind of an indestructible deathlessness. Also the person can achieve a rainbow body by transforming the body into a mass of light. So all this depends on the control that a person has over *rlung*.

At first, one starts with mantra. One will visualize the body as the body of a deity, whether as Vajrayogini or Vajrapani, etc. Then the person will recite the mantra and concentrate the mind. In the person's heart there will be a seed syllable with the mantra surrounding it. By focusing the mind on the seed syllable and reciting the mantra, the *rlung* will be controlled.

Here we will observe two kinds of *rlung*: one that will cleanse all kinds of past wrongdoings and obscurations and the other for preventing sickness. First we will consider the *rlung* that will cleanse the wrong-doings, obscurations and the conflicting emotions. There are nine kinds of breath divided into three subdivisions of three. In the early hour of the morning, as soon as we get up, we can all do the following: sit cross-legged in the vajra or lotus position, straightening the body and the back. We have mainly three kinds of emotional poisons. The first is passion, the second is aggression and the third is dullness or stupidity. So by doing this *rlung* exercise, we are appeasing the three emotional poisons from conflict at a particular time.

So we will consider the first breath and passion or desire. On the first breath we inhale, we block the left nostril and inhale by the right. Then we breathe strong and drive the air through the naval. When we have finished inhaling strongly and have driven the air down to the navel, we hold the breath down. Passion is symbolized by the bird. We imagine that all our desires are taking the form of this bird and visualize it. When we are holding our breath, the air goes down to the genitals and then it comes out through the left channel. At that time we start to exhale through the left nostril, with our passion in the form of a bird, and it dissolves into the earth and is appeased. We do this exercise three times for appeasing passion.

The next three breaths are relating to pacifying anger. The animal that symbolizes anger is the snake. So we breathe by blocking the right nostril and breathing in through the left nostril. At the same time we visualize our anger in the form of snakes. Then at the time of exhaling, we will block the left nostril and have the breath come out of the body through the right channel, through the right nostril. All our anger, in the form of snakes, will dissolve into the earth. We do this breathing exercise three times.

The last three breath exercises are to pacify ignorance or dullness. The animal connected to this is the pig. We have to imagine very small, tiny pigs that symbolize our ignorance. When we inhale, we inhale through both nostrils and then bring the breath down to the navel. Then we visualize innumerable small pigs. We should not imagine at this point that we have two nostrils. We should imagine that we have only one channel. Holding the breath or air in the navel for some time, we will have to bring out all these small pigs which symbolize our ignorance and dullness and stupidity through this one orifice. After they come out of this one channel, they will dissolve into the earth. Then we feel that we have vanquished ignorance or dullness. So we do three breathing exercises thrice in their respective ways.

By practicing these breathing exercises, from the Buddhist or spiritual point of view, we are cleansing our being of the three poisons of passion, aggression and ignorance. We also say that all diseases have their origin or root in these three poisonous emotions. From a spiritual point of view or from a hygienic point of view, we are cleansing our being of emotional poisons as well as physical diseases.

Q. Do the three humors change according to the growth of a person?
A. Yes they do. The three humors do change according to their growth into a stalk, blooms flower and so forth; the three humors are there from the very beginning of conception. However, the predominance of the three humors varies from childhood to old age.

At the time of childhood, the predominant humor is *bad-kan* or phlegm. A child is kind of fleshy when it is born. It is whitish and is attracted to sweet things. This is the sign of a predominance of *bad-kan*.

When the child grows, the flesh formation changes. The beauty of the child changes. The flesh does not remain the same. The features do not remain the same. The child grows into adolescence and *mkhris-pa* or bile takes predominance over the other humors. At this time, the person will be more prone to becoming proud, angry and restless. He or she will be attracted to sour things, to uncooked things, and also like kind of food that is not very rich.

Then the last part of the life of a person, when they reach old age, then they are considered as a *rlung* person. This means the person will naturally change. The flesh will change and begin to have wrinkles. And the person's mind will be more prone to the influence of *rlung*. That means even if he or she was a peaceful person before, they will change into a short-tempered person. When the person is young he or she is prone to pride, competitiveness and adventurism. As they grow old, they become nervous of competition and measure each step much more carefully. The person has more doubts, more thought and therefore, is more worried. This raises the *rlung* and because of that he or she becomes more short-tempered in old age. We are talking about 60 years onwards. Then the person will be more attracted to substantious food, for example, meat, alcohol like beer and hard liquor. This is a natural manifestation in the being, in the lifetime of a person and in connection with the three humors of *rlung*, *mkhris-pa* and *bad-kan*.

7

Relationship Between Body, Speech and Mind

We are meeting at the Kosmos today, we are meeting here so that we can talk about Tibetan medicine and culture. And to all of you who did not come yesterday, and all of you who did come yesterday, I extend my greetings.

Today, according to what has been arranged, we are going to discuss the relationship between body, speech and mind. We will also discuss karma and reincarnation, the relationship between Tibetan medicine and Buddhism, and so on. We will try to cover all these topics according to the time we have.

When we say body we actually mean the five outer elements and the five inner elements. When these come together, that is what we call body. The five outer elements with which the body is formed are earth, water, fire, air and space. These outer elements aid or help the inner elements which are wood, fire, iron, earth and water. When the five outer elements come in connection with the five inner elements, combining and mutually helping each other, then this human body is formed. This human body is conceived and starts to form in the womb.

What is cause for the body to be formed? The main cause is ignorance. What is this ignorance? What this ignorance consists of is ignorance with respect to the self. Where there is no ego, or independent self, one assumes an independent self, an ego. Where there are no enemies in relation to other beings, then we assume enemies. When we are talking about assuming an ego in oneself, if we take a look at the five outer and inner elements of the body, we will see clearly that we can not assume an ego in the outer and inner elements of the body. For instance, when we are talking about our body with its five main organs and the six hollow organs, we always refer to it as "mine." We say, "this is my kidney," "these are my lungs." However, when there is death or even an operation in which the kidney is extracted, at that time we can not say "my kidney." It is no longer "mine." There is no labelling of an "I" in that kidney.

So far we have considered how we assume an ego in our body and its parts as 'mine.' This can be applied also to objects like a watch or a bag which we assume as 'mine.' When such objects are lost or destroyed, we can no longer assume the objects as ours. It has already gone into the sphere of nothingness.

Let us discuss when we imagine or assume we have enemies when actually there are no enemies. If we examine minutely, we will realize that there is not even one being that we can truly consider to be our enemy. Why is this so? In this one particular lifetime now, we might see that a person does not like us and we consider him or her an enemy. However, when this life ends and another life begins, then we may have a relationship with this person either as our father or mother. As such we have no basis to consider any person as our enemy now because in some other lifetime, we have either been father, mother, son or daughter of one another. So if we examine carefully, we have taken numerous births and rebirths in this world. I can say I am a Tibetan but I have been born in many lifetimes in Holland, Australia or Africa. Other people, who are Dutch or Indian now, have been born in innumerable places including Tibet and so forth. We can go throughout the world and we can examine various rebirths and come to this realization that the whole world is not our enemy as we have been citizens of the whole world in one lifetime or other.

Now we will talk about speech. Speech is that which communicates and conveys messages. It is the spokesman of the body and mind. For instance, if the mind is happy we convey this happiness by jokes, songs or laughter. If we are very angry, then we convey our wrath by abuse or argument.

We will not talk about the mind, the experience of the mind and how the speech conveys the state of the mind. Let us consider which are the particular unhappinesses or sufferings of the mind. For instance, if we say 'I am very happy today', or 'Today I am unhappy as I did not get the thing I really wanted,' these kind of worries or unhappinesses exist only in the mind; they do not pertain to the body. Then we express these kinds of feelings through speech, which acts as a spokesman of the mind. Sometimes we have problems with the body. We might have headache. We have pain in one of the organs like liver or joints. Such pains we can express. We can say, "I have pains in the joints.' Speech, in this case, is working as a spokesman of the body.

With body, speech and mind, we can act. We can act either virtuously or also we can create wrongdoings. We will start by analyzing what are the wrongdoings according to Buddhism.

There are three types of wrongdoings connected with body. The first one is to kill, to take someone's life. The second is to steal or take what is not given. The third one is sexual misconduct. These three are called the wrongdoings of the body. There are different intensities in each of these actions according to whether four conditions are met or not.

In the case of killing, then, we can kill inadvertently. We can also kill by fulfilling these four conditions: having an object that is to be killed, the intention to kill it, the action of killing and then at the end the result of killing. And also when we kill inadvertently, there are degrees of intensity in the act.

Let us cite an example fulfilling the four conditions of killing. We have a pig. From the time of its birth till its growth into a fully mature pig, we feed this pig, not because we want to help it out of kindness, but with the idea to kill it at some point. So that is the object that we wish to kill. The thought or the intention of killing it is the second stage. When we want to eat the meat, we decide to kill and prepare it to be killed. The actual killing would be the third step and this would involve killing it by choking or stabbing. And the fourth stage is concluding the act by cooking and eating the meat. We feel satisfied by eating it, and therefore the four conditions of this action have been completed to a full extent. So when one eats meat, we cannot say that there is nothing wrong with it. However, the wrongdoing of eating meat can be lessened. The act can be brought to a light negative influence if one does not eat meat in order to satisfy pleasure or gross desire for eating meat, but to improve the weakness of the body and improve one's health, in order to serve other people who are less fortunate and stuck in misery of one kind or another. So if one can infuse the mind with such thoughts when eating meat, the negative aspect of the act can be lessened considerably.

Let us now discuss stealing. There are many ways to steal. The first one we will consider is to steal surreptitiously. The second way of stealing is by confusing or deceiving the other person. The third way of stealing is to use power, like a bandit or armed robber, and endanger the lives of other in order to steal or rob.

Let us now see the three wrongdoings of speech. The first wrongdoing of speech is abusive language like, for instance, to call people names, to be heartless to someone else saying, 'You are a pig' and so on. The second wrongdoing is senseless talk. Senseless talk in general I think all of us do, but particularly most of all myself as I have to give many lectures. So, if one does not have the right intention when one is talking, then it becomes a wrongdoing of the speech. The worst kind of senseless talk is the actual senseless talk—saying whatever comes in mind, one thing after another, just like that, without any coherence or sense.

There are three wrongdoings of the action of the mind. The first one is covetousness, to covet or to have greed, to want to possess something that is not yours. This wrongdoing concerns the desire to possess something that belongs to someone else. For example, if a woman sees that another woman is wearing very beautiful jewelry then this thought arises that 'Oh! If these jewels were mine I would be so happy.' This desire or greed which actually comes to our mind is covetousness, and this is probably one that comes very naturally in all of us.

The second type of wrongdoing is to have a harmful mind or a desire to harm someone else. Mostly this comes from envy or jealousy. For example, in school if someone else is very successful and we think of harming him or her by obstructing their studies, by stealing their books, etc. This desire to harm another person is a wrongdoing of the mind.

We will next consider wrong views. There are two types of wrong views: ordinary wrong views and extraordinary wrong views. Ordinary wrong view would be to have wrong views or attitudes against one's parents or teachers and the like. These days this wrong view is very common and widespread. It is because the character of the children does not go along with the character of their parents, causing a number of frictions and problems, and many children so easily forget the full kindness of their parents. Therefore, the children always quarrel with their parents, who are full of kindness. We may be gaining more information and improving our academic standards day by day, but if we do not maintain this relationship of kindness with our parents in a healthy way then when we ourselves have children, because of the force of karma, it is likely that we will have the same problems with our children that we had with our parents.

Now we will consider the extraordinary wrong views. They are in accordance with one's own religion. Each country or each region has its own religion. Generally speaking, in Tibet we had the Buddhist religion. In Tibet we are Buddhists, but in India they are mostly Hindus and in the West there are mostly Christians. So we speak in terms of the religion pursued by every individual. Then in all of these religions, there are a lot of teachings about helping others, about protecting others and about devoting one's energies in order to become liberated. If one lacks complete faith in one's own religion, that is a wrong view. Even if one can not actually practice religion, to have the faith to acknowledge this religion as one's religion is what is necessary. Breaking this faith would be committing an extraordinary wrong action having a wrong view.

According to the Buddhist view, the results of our actions will determine our rebirth in our next life, our form of existence. As we have described, there are wrong actions and there are virtuous actions. According to the actions that we have committed, six types of existences are possible. Six types of rebirth are possible. The six types of beings are not all born out of the womb like a humans. There are three types of birth. For instance, all humans are born out of a womb. Worms and other types of insects are born out of a combination of warmth and humidity. One state of existence is the god-realm; in this realm many of the gods are born as if out of flowers, miraculous types of birth.

These six states of beings can be further divided into happy and miserable states. Each of these two can be further sub-divided into three each. The three higher states are the states of gods, of *asuras* or jealous gods and then humans. From these three, the human body is the best as it is the greatest opportunity for attaining liberation from existence. Gods and jealous gods look upon the human body as something they would like to obtain. Yet humans look upon the body of gods as something they would like to obtain.

The lower realms or the realms of miserable existence are

animals, hungry spirits or ghosts and the hell realm. If we are to examine the sufferings of each of these beings in the six realms, it would take many days. So let us mention only the gross sufferings of each that characterize their state.

The main suffering of the realm of gods is that of death, of disintegration and of falling down since any other birth is lower than theirs. These beings, these gods, when they come close to their hour of dying, begin to show certain death signs in their bodies. For instance, the garland of flowers which they wear withers and their bodies start to stink and so forth. So they are left alone and neglected by their companions, by their friends. During the whole time of their life, they have the faculty to see where they are going to be reborn. This extraordinary perception brings them a tremendous sense of regret and pain when they see that they are going to be reborn as a donkey or a monkey. So this whole process of awaiting death and knowing beforehand that they are going to be reborn either in the animal or hell realm is very painful. It causes them a great deal of mental suffering. This is their main suffering.

The main suffering of the jealous gods comes from fighting wars. The fighting comes about because the gods of one level possess a kind of wish-fulfilling tree. The roots of this tree are in the realm of the jealous gods but the fruit of the tree is in the realm of the gods. Then each one claims that the tree belongs to their own sphere. Because of this dispute they always fight, the gods and the jealous gods. This brings about great pain and is the main suffering that the *asuras* or the jealous gods must undergo. In the fighting the *asuras* can not win; they are always defeated. The gods like Indira and Brahma possess a wheel which makes them invincible in fighting the wars.

In the human realm we know what kinds of suffering we experience. Just as we experience suffering, we should also realize that the *asuras* and the gods also experience their particular sufferings which they can not escape. In the human realm, the four main sufferings that we can mention are birth, old age, sickness and death. The suffering of birth takes place at the moment of birth. When a child is being born it feels as if a rope were passed through a very thin hole of a needle, and it feels as if all the flesh and bones in the body are completely pressed. After the child is born, whenever something touches the skin the child feels it as very coarse, as if it were kept on a bed of thorns.

The suffering of old age is a process that takes many years. For example, when we are children our flesh is very strong and bright, without even a single wrinkle at all. During youth, the person has his or her own strength. They sets off to do whatever they wish and at that time there is great pride because the person is a youth and feels mature. Women at that point in life will experience the suffering of giving birth. When old age overtakes us, we will see that our face has changed, our teeth have fallen out, we have many more wrinkles, the hair has grown grey and so forth. These different signs of ageing bring unhappiness in the mind and that is a human suffering. This suffering of growing old comes to most of us and this suffering stays for a long time.

Now we will talk about sickness. This suffering of sickness comes whether one is a child, a youth or an old man or woman. From a simple cold up to cancer, there are all the range of sickness that we know about. In addition to the basic pain of birth, old age and death, there are two important characteristics of this suffering of sickness. When one is sick, one has to take medicine which one does not want to take. A patient may hate the medicine but it is compulsory to take it. The patient may not like to have part of his or her internal organs extracted or replaced through surgery, as is common in Western medicine. Yet the patient has no choice, really. In our system, the patient would have to undergo moxa or fire treatment and chew hand-made pills. These are the added sufferings that come from sickness. The second added suffering of being sick is that a family has to spend a lot of precious money that was saved through hardwork. If a sickness is very difficult to cure and it takes a long time, then the patient has to spend a great deal of money in order to recover. So the patient and his or her family members will suffer seeing a fortune being dissipated in this manner.

Finally, there is the suffering of death. There are two kinds of sufferings of death that we will see. There is the suffering of a fierce kind of death and the suffering of a mild kind of death. For a person who has engaged in virtuous activities during his or her lifetime, when death comes the person will just think that he or she is going somewhere else. They will not be afraid and will not have much mental suffering. In this category we will also include death by accident, when life abruptly comes to an end. In such deaths there is not much mental anguish as everything happens very suddenly. However, in the case of a sickness of terminal nature, the patient suffers tremendous mental anguish, as if the heart is pierced by a knife.

The last type of suffering concerns the death of a person who has engaged in immoral conduct throughout his or her life and has not observed practice for their own inner development. For such a person, when the signs of death appears, he or she will have a very tormented time when it will seem as if the person is being attacked by many devils with weapons from all around, and so on.

8
Rebirth

We have seen now, very briefly, about the connection between the body, speech and mind. Let us now talk about rebirth. There are many kinds of rebirth. Today we will examine only two kinds. We will examine the person or being who is reborn as a result of his or her karma or actions of the previous life. One is reborn by the action of his or her own respective karma. It is not something that comes from nowhere, without any cause. One takes this rebirth strictly as a result of the actions undertaken in a previous lifetime. If during this lifetime one pursues good actions purely devoted towards helping others, it will help to obtain a human form in the next life. It would bring a shower of the blessings of a good, pleasant and prosperous family, in accordance with the actions one has committed in the previous birth. There are many types of places where one can be reborn. Some places are extremely hot. Some are extremely cold. Some are temperate while others are infertile or fertile. Each person takes his or her rebirth in these places according to the karma collected in the previous birth. A person of good karma will be reborn in a place that is not too hot or cold and where food is abundant. If one wishes to be reborn in such a place, one should accumulate good karma, engage in positive actions and maintain good morality. By the force of such actions and the desire to be reborn in such a place under such special circumstances, one will be reborn in such a place. Such outer conditions are called external or circumstantial conditions.

Now let us talk about the inner qualifications that pertain to oneself and not to the surroundings. Such a person of inner qualities is one who will have all the six senses unimpaired. He or she will have faith in religion, will be humble in dealings and respectful of elders. All the qualities of a positive person will be present. Everybody wishes for his or her happiness, but that does not happen. Not everybody is happy. In fact, most are unhappy, suffering from one misery or the other. This is because what one actually gets does not often go strictly in accordance with one's wishes, but is the result of one's karma—the result of actions that one has committed in a previous birth. So the rebirth one takes is strictly in accordance with one's karma. It is not something that one can choose. And to be born in a place that has difficult circumstances like lack of water and food, difficult climate and so forth, these are also fixed by one's karma and there is nothing that we can do, there is no choice. In terms of one's own characteristics, which are the result of one's positive and negative karma, one can be born with a body that is crippled or have problems with one's organs or be blind and deaf, and so on. These are the different characteristics which show that the person has accumulated negative karma in one's previous life.

Also the sex that one is born into is due to one's karma. There are three types of women: one is merely woman, the other is intermediate woman and the third is extremely fine female. And then there is also the hermaphrodite.

For instance, a woman who is classified as merely woman is one whose sex is female but the different parts of the body, like the face, looks like that of a male, and the skin is rough and hairy. Even if she wants to have a baby, she can not conceive. If someone hears her speak but does not see her, they would think a man is talking, as her voice is very masculine. Most of her voice will come not through the mouth but through the nose.

The intermediate woman, is like all of us women gathered here. None of us, including myself, is a superior woman. We are classified as such because our face and our whole body is merely feminine, our voice is the voice of a woman and we can talk through our mouths. Moreover we all have the ability, the faculties, to procreate. Thus we are intermediate woman. A middle type of woman, such as ourselves, when relating to other persons, are sometimes liked and sometimes not liked.

Now let us talk about the supreme kind of very special woman, who is called extremely fine woman. Her hair will be of fixed length and reach just down to her waist without growing further. It shortens itself and there is no need to cut it. She will be tall, her height will be exactly the length of the full stretch of her two arms. The hair will also be black with a bluish hue. Her complexion will be light like the moon, without any spots. The eyes of such a woman will be long and big and the eyebrows will be naturally thin. The cheeks will be naturally red like an apple, without having to makeup. The teeth will be like a garland of pearls. She will have exactly 32 teeth. The neck will be five fingers long. Her shoulders, her chest and the waist will be very very thin. Her breasts will be smallish. They will not be falling down or be too big. Her speech will be such that when one listens to her one is automatically attracted to her talk and wishes to hear more. It will be like, for instance, when one plays a special melody on the flute for the deer and the deer automatically feel attracted to the melody. In that way, her speech is so pleasant that it would attract all beings. Such a woman is liked by everybody.

So, we have discussed all the kinds of women. Let us examine men now. Let us start by the superior kind of man. The supreme man should be tall. His height should be exactly the same length as his two arms extended. The complexion of this man will not be completely white, but be a little bit reddish. His forehead will have the shape of the moon. The cheeks, as we say in the Tibetan tradition, will be like that of a snow lion. The eyes should not be longish, but more round and big. The four canine teeth should be a little bit pronounced. The molar teeth will have three roots instead of two, which means that the person will not have problems with his teeth even at an advanced age. Naturally, this person will always sit straight like a falcon. He will not be bent down. He will have great strength, skill and ability with his hands. For instance, in Tibet, if this person practices archery then he will never miss the target because he can aim perfectly with the hands. Such a person, if he runs, he will be first, and also if he rides a horse then he will always be first. If he swims in a river, like the strong rivers we have in Tibet, then the river will fail to divert him and he will be able to keep his direction straight. When he talks people will not be bored at what he has to say, but they will laugh, be pleased, and have a very nice time. When he writes or when he calculates, he will not make mistakes. His family members will like and respect him. This is a superior man.

Now the intermediate man: there are many different kinds, but I will mention his characteristics very briefly. This person will know how to talk, how to write, how to add, but he will make mistakes. If he practices archery or some other skill, then he will mostly hit the target but then there will also be time when he is not able to, but mostly he will hit and win. In relationship with other people he will have both kinds of receptivity; some people will like him, some will not.

Now let's talk about the lowest kind of man. His face will look like a woman's. His way of talking will also be feminine. His expression, his whole way of moving and expressing himself, will be very feminine. He will lack courage or bravery when he has to face certain difficult situation. In his relationship with the circle of his family, he will be disliked by most people and liked by a few.

All these different characteristics, whether it is superior, middling, or lowest kind of a man or a woman, all of these things are not inculcated by oneself, but are the result of one's own past karma.

Let's talk about the hermaphrodite. There is also a kind of neutral hermaphrodite. The first hermaphrodite goes in accordance with the definition of a hermaphrodite. The second one is a person who changes into a hermaphrodite. The definition of a hermaphrodite is that, from the time of birth, he has both types of genitals. He will have male sex organs above the female sex organ. Nowadays there are many cases like this. The right breast will be flat like a man's, but the left breast will be like a woman's. One the body this person will have a lot of hair. Sometimes his voice will sound like a woman and sometimes it will sound like a man. Since the ability to procreate does not exist in him, then he will not be able to cause a child in a woman or to bear a child as a woman does.

The other type of hermaphrodite, that of change or transformation into a hermaphrodite, is the case of a person who physically looks exactly like a man, even possessing the male sex organs. For six months, he will be completely like a man, he will act like a man and he will do everything as a man does. However, for the next six months, although he has the body of a man, his whole mind becomes more like a woman's; he will like what women like, he will feel as they do.

So, based on one's karma, this is the way one's body is acquired. When two people are very connected through friendship and other types of bonds, when they keep their bond in a very healthy way, then it is very likely that in a future lifetime these people will be born as twins.

9
Buddhism and Medicine

What we have been talking about up to now is in accordance with Buddhism. Now let's talk about the connection between Buddhism and Tibetan medicine. When we examine the Tibetan medical system, the medical authors who have written the texts, the doctors who practice the system and so forth, everything has a relationship with the Dharma. The Dharma is the Buddhist religion. The basic texts, the authoritative texts of Tibetan medical science have all come from the Buddha of Medicine. There is not one basic text that has not been propounded by him. This explains the connection between the authoritative medical texts and Buddhism.

Second is the connection between the medicine itself and Buddhism. The first medicines that came into existence are the three kinds of fruits which are called *aaru*, *baru* and *kyuru*. These three medicines are able to benefit diseases coming from *rlung*, *mkhris-pa* and *bad-kan*. How these medicines came into existence also has reference to Buddhism. The legend goes that the first person who planted these medicines in this world was a woman. This woman was an emanation of the goddess called Dusolmah and came into being through the blessings of Buddha. She undertook all kinds of hardships in order to collect these seeds and to plant these seeds in this world. Then she went into the realm of the gods, the heavenly abode and from there took the seeds of the five kinds of *arurah*. The *Arurah* that she started out with a called *arurah namgyal* or completely victorious myrobalan. That medicine alone has five tastes in itself. Of the six kinds of flavors or tastes the only one that is lacking is salty, all the other tastes are possessed by *arurah namgyal*. This completely victorious myrobalan fruit, when it existed in the realm of the gods where a healing system or medical system already existed, looked like the head of a horse. In the legends of Tibetan medicine much is written about the means Yitrogma, the emanation of the goddess Dusolma, applied to obtain this fruit from India and Brahma, the two gods. The wife of god Indra was the one who gave the completely victorious myrobalan to Yitrogma.

After bringing the seed of the fruit to the human world, she planted it first in Bodh Gaya. At the time of planting she made many kinds of wishes. She started off by making wishes in the eastern direction of Vajrasattva, Dorje Sempa in Tibetan, who is an embodiment of the Buddha and who aids in cleansing wrongdoings and obscurations. So she prayed that this plant would be able to cleanse wrongdoings and obscurations. Then, facing the western direction and with folded hands, she prayed to Buddha Amitaba. To Amitaba she prayed that this fruit may bring long-life to whoever eats it. Towards the south she prayed with folded hands to the Buddha Ratnasambhava. She prayed that may this fruit have the ability to bring riches and fortune. In the north she prayed to Amogasidhi that whoever partakes of this myrobalan may have a body that is indestructible like the vajra, a body that does not age, does not decay, and is always firm and strong.

When the seed of myrobalan was planted five branches came out from the tree. From these five branches a great number of leaves came. The central branch yielded the *arurah* called completely victorious myrobalan. Another branch yielded another type of *arurah* called golden or yellow type of *arurah*. Another branch yielded another type of *arurah* called *longsih*. Another branch yielded an *arurah* called *kempo*, which is a dry *arurah*. Then the fifth branch yielded the last type of *arurah* which is called *arurah* with seven foldings.

The central *arurah*, or completely victorious myrobalan, is able to cure diseases of *rlung*, *mkhris-pa* and *bad-kan*. Nowadays what we are able to use is only the four other types of *arurah*. We can only use this central *arurah* out of great blessing. We must have great blessing and luck to find it because it is so rare. It is difficult to find because in our time, which is considered a time of decadence, this fruit does not grow anymore.

Each time a world teacher, a Buddha comes to this world, four special things happen. One is that this *arurah* grows at the same time. Secondly a special kind of flower grows that comes only when a Buddha comes. Then, a universal kind of emperor, who has a special wheel to transport him anywhere he wishes, comes to rule the world. The last sign is a special kind of horse, which can bring the emperor to any place, takes birth. These things can exist after a universal teacher like the Buddha comes to this world. When the time of decadence comes these things disappear. Now we are in this time of decadence. Nowadays kings or emperors have to take a plane or go in car. They lack this magic wheel.

In the *thangka* paintings, the Buddha of Medicine is holding a bowl. And inside the bowl is this completely victorious *arurah* which does not grow nowadays. When we make medicine nowadays, we use the other four types of *arurah* after performing ritual which will bring the nectar from the visualized from of the Buddha of Medicine on the *arurah*. This amrita or nectar will fall from the bowl of the Medicine Buddha. The *arurah* we are using will take the characteristics of the completely victorious *arurah* when the nectar falls on it. So it is more or less the same. The Buddha of Medicine sits in Vajrasanna. His elbows are touching his waist and his middle finger is touching the earth. When this middle finger can touch the earth in this way it is a sign that the person has refrained from stealing or taking what was not freely given for innumerable lifetimes. None of us is able to touch the ground in that way because probably none of us is free from that kind of wrongdoing. When we were children and we wanted some chocolate then we would just take some and go, no?

This is the legend of how the *arurah* was brought from the realm of the gods to the human world. Concerning the subject of the connection between Buddhism and Tibetan medicine, we have completed the discussion on category of the medicine of fruit *arurah* and how this particular ingredient of medicine had received the blessing of Medicine Buddha.

Now we will examine another category of medicine which comes from jewels. For this type of medicine, the emanation of goddess Dusolma called Yitrogma is important. She went to the country of the *nagas*. It is not easy for humans to go to such a country because the human body is impure and it stinks in a certain way which harms the *nagas*. So it is not possible for a human to reach the *nagas* easily. Because of this, the goddess told a certain holy man that she intended to go to the country of the *nagas* alone in order to obtain medicine made from jewels. However, she needed to know the way to go to the *nagas* so she asked for special oral instructions as to how she should proceed. Because her intention was to benefit all sentient beings, this holy man told her that he would help her to go there. He gave her a protective wheel with which she would be immune to the poisonous breath of the *nagas*. She would also be free from harm, and also be free from danger in her encounter with the *nagas*.

After making aspiration prayers to Buddha, she set out for the ocean. Then she reached the place where the king of *nagas* had his palace. On reaching this palace, she found that it was surrounded by a moat which was full of poisonous snakes. Guarding the entrance door were two guardians. They were *nagas* whose lower part of the body looked like snakes and their heads looked human, and then on top of their heads there were the heads of seven snakes. In their folded hands they held precious jewels. In order to traverse this moat full of poisonous snakes, Yitrogma did a breathing practice that enabled her to go over it. She could not go straight into the castle after doing this meditation, but she got quite a ways into the palace. When the *nagas* smelled the smell of a human, then they all came to see who was there. They found this woman who was extremely beautiful and captivating. That is actually the meaning of her name—Yitrogma. This means that whoever sees her, their mind automatically becomes attracted to her, because of her exceeding beauty. So, the queens, the consorts of the kings, as soon as they saw her, they became very jealous and they decided to give her poison. Then, one of the queens breathed out this black kind of poison which completely covered Yitrogma. Because of this poison she fell down and lost consciousness. Then, after a few minutes, she came to her senses and she was just as she had been before, unharmed. Then there was a great commotion and a lot of noise was created there in the palace. So when the kings heard all this noise they came to see what was happening. When they saw Yigtrogma they immediately became attracted to her.

    The *naga* king, because he was so captivated by her beauty, told her that if she would become his consort then he would give her any jewel she wanted. Out of a wish to help all sentient beings, Yitrogma stayed with this king of *nagas* for a few days. Because of this, she could receive, as an offering from the king, many kinds of jewels. After she received these, then she returned to the human world.

    Most of the jewels that we use nowadays come from the ocean in the way that we have explained. According to our tradition, most of the jewels that come out of the water are very good for treating of diseases like leprosy and other skin diseases which have connection to the action of *nagas*. Therefore, whenever one makes medicine to treat cases like leprosy then we usually use precious substances which originated in water.

Now we will talk about herbal medicine. Herbal medicine is also connected with Buddhism because of the kindness, the compassion, and the blessings of the Buddha. All the power, compassion, and knowledge of the Buddhas are embodied in three main expressions. One is Manjushri, who embodies wisdom, Avalokiteshvara, who embodies love and compassion and Vajrapani, who embodies power.

Dealing with the first kind of herbal medicines, tradition explains that when the tears of Majushri fell on the earth, then from these tears was born a kind of medicinal plant. It measures one stretched hand high and has many yellow flowers. These flowers have many dewdrops on them which do not dry out even when the sun is right on them.

The same is the legend as Avalokiteshvara, who embodies compassion and love, and is constantly freeing beings from the miserable realms. Yet his work is never ending as newcomers to this miserable realm keep increasing every day. So, then because of his compassion and deep feeling for the suffering of all these beings, he cried and the tears, when they fell to the earth, sprouted a plant which is called the tears of Avalokiteshvara. This is a white kind of herb which is one of the most precious ingredients of Tibetan medicine.

And the same legend continues with Vajrapani. Through his tears were born a dark blue kind of herb which is a bit thick and stronger than the preceding two. This also has dewdrops that do not dry.

In the same way there are medicines that come from animals or from other sentient beings, for instance the musk comes from the musk deer. This also has its root as a blessing from enlightened beings. In this one case, there was a Bodhisattva, or a being who is intent on enlightenment for the benefit of others. This being was sick with leprosy again and again. He said it is time for me to die, but at the time of death I pray that from my body, flesh, blood, and all that goes in the earth, herbs may grow that will be able to treat leprosy. With his flesh he specially blessed one of the four types of *arurah* that we talked about before, which is the golden colored *arurah*. This medicine has the same kind of nutrition and strength as meat. From his bones then the blessing went to the medicine called *ruta*. It is a root. When it is taken and broken up, the inside root looked like bone. From his tendon then also another root was created which is very sweet smelling and has many kind of filaments. With his blood he blessed the navel of certain deers, which created this medicinal substance which is called musk. The navel of the musk deer is not like an ordinary navel, like the human navels that do not have any special qualities. These special deer create in the navel the musk used in medicine, which came through the bless of the blood of this Bodhisattva.

From the kinds of medicines which are derived from stone, there is one called *chang-she*. Thang thong Gyalpo, a great *mahasiddha* of Tibet became sick and was ready to pass away. So many celestial beings and *dakinis* came from all the four directions. Five *dakinis* from the four directions and the center came and brought this medicine called *chang-she*, which has the nature of stone, and brought it to him, saying, for the benefit of all sentient beings, please accept this. Taking this medicine, he stayed a longer time without dying. This medicine is one of those that are especially blessed. Another name for this medicine is *drubtog rilkar*. It is the white pill of an enlightened being. With this medicine one is able to cure even one hundred diseases in one body. Now we have also seen a medicine which was blessed by *dakinis*, the celestial beings.

In this way, we can examine all the hundreds and hundreds of types of medicines that are derived from herbs, minerals and animals like deer and go into the origin of each. Let us now put all this information in one point.

There are certain differences between Tibetan and Western medicine in terms of preparation, in terms of its diagnosis, and then in the identification of the disease and the check-up of diagnose. A Tibetan doctor, after contemplating on the difficulty and rarity of obtaining this human body which has all the opportunities of attaining liberation, will consider and be convinced that it is a rare and unique opportunity to have this human body in which he or she is a doctor at this particular time. The doctor thinks that if they are not going to use this body to help others who are suffering, who are sick and need medicine to be cured, then they will die. They will lose this body and will probably never get the opportunity to help other beings in this way. This is the way a Tibetan doctor thinks, the way he or she sets the aims and intention. This attitude may differ a little from a Western doctor.

The second difference may be in the way of dealing with the patient. When a Tibetan doctor is facing the patient, he or she thinks that in many lifetimes this person has been my mother or father and therefore has shown me kindness. It does not matter at this moment what the nationality, race, or religion the patient is. He may be Muslim, or Christian, Communist, Buddhist, or whatever, and the doctor relates to the patient with that kindness, remembering the kindness that the patient has shown in some other lifetime. Then the doctor treats the patient, and that therapy will be done through love and care. A Western doctor, by training, is not required to possess such an attitude.

In preparing the medicine, we do not directly add the ingredients in many cases. For instance, if we are using precious jewels, these jewels have to be detoxified; they possess certain kinds of impurities that must be cleansed. If we are using turquoise for certain medicines, then we will grind it into a powder and then it has to go through three different stages that will cleanse it from three impure effects on the human body. To make the pill correctly we will mix 20 or 25 different ingredients together with the turquoise, according to the medical texts. All of these ingredients are considered to be blessed by an enlightened being, by a Buddha, and then they are prepared and made into one pill. The attitude which the doctor must have toward this medicine is that, since the ingredients of this medicine have been blessed by Buddha, the medicines will not only cure the patient from the three diseases of *rlung*, *mkhris-pa* and *bad-kan* but will also extend the patient's life and finally become the seed for the patient to realize the importance of obtaining enlightenment for the benefit of others and to reach the supreme state of Buddhahood. This medicine is like a blessing which enters into the stream of the patient's being. In Tibet, where the distances between communities are vast and there is no means of easy communication with a person who lives in a place where there is no doctor, taking just one such pill as a blessing from the Buddha is done in the case of serious illness or before death.

The treatment in Tibetan medicine is usually a soft treatment of the disease. When medicine is given to cure the specific disease, then also the side effects that this medicine can bring about are also considered. So there is a vast way of considering the problem of disease. The technique of healing covers more than the particular disease that the person is experiencing because it considers eliminating the side effects at the same time. In Tibetan medical science, we seldom use drastic techniques like operation and so forth. We usually attack the disease with a soft or gentle method.

Finally, when the patient has already been cured from the disease by a particular doctor, then a relationship grows between that particular doctor and that patient; I will talk a little bit about that. If during the treatment the doctor shows himself or herself to be very greedy, interested in money, lacking gentleness in the therapy and subjecting the patient to hard treatment, then even if the patient is cured he or she will feel aversion toward the doctor afterwards because he remembers the negative aspects of the doctor. That means that although the patient's life was saved, he or she does not remember the doctor as a symbol of kindness and compassion.

In my particular case, I have a private clinic in Dharamsala where I have many different kinds of patients coming to me. If they can pay for their medicine I take the fees, because I have to buy the different ingredients and that costs money. Usually I give medicines free of costs to all monks from all the sects. If a patient who comes who does not have the money to pay because he or she is poor, that is also alright. I still give the medical treatment. The important thing, in any case, is that the relationship between the patient and the doctor remains a good one, a pure one.

It might seem a bit strange to you how we Tibetan doctors approach the topic of diagnosis because we do not use the aid of electronic equipments, we do not use sophisticated implements in order to diagnose a patient. What do we use? A doctor in his or her own being has these five elements corresponding naturally to the patient's five elements, and which can measure through the touch of the patient. That is the means of diagnosis, in which both beings come into contact naturally, without any gadgets. When we talk about natural medicine which is made with natural ingredients, then it may be that it does not help the disease but it also means that it cannot harm the patient, either. This has been pronounced by the Medicine Buddha Himself and by a great number of learned scholars and practitioners of medicine. This is also my own experience. From one's own experience, we can see that this is true.

In Tibet, because I belong to a family of doctors called Khangkar known in the Kyirong region where we lived, the people had great confidence and faith because everything was organized for a long, long time. Then when we had to come to India as ordinary refugees, there was nothing special about us. People did not have that kind of recognition, and when I started I had to start all over again. Many people, the first Indian patients when they came to see me said, 'Well! You come from such a cold place, maybe your medicine is heat-producing and if this is given to me in India maybe it will be harmful to me.' They had that kind of doubt or apprehension. After more than a decade of practice we can say that all Indians have complete faith in our medical system. Not just ordinary people, but also doctors show confidence and belief in Tibetan medical science. Every day, if I am not tired, I examine from one to two hundred patients.

Today I have talked briefly about the Tibetan medical system and how it has an origin which is valid and which is genuine. If a system does not have a genuine origin than it is not of great use. Whatever is related to the connection between Buddhism and medicine is included in the Third Tantra, which is called the *Tantra of Oral Instructions*. For instance, whenever one has a disease then one can cure the disease oneself by recitation of specific mantras. It can be done by one's own effort.

Certain lamas have the power of curing a patient by their recitation of a mantra. In the Tibetan tradition, when a person visits a lama then it is customary to come for his blessing. The blessing is called 'empowerment of the hand' in Tibetan. It is not an actual, complete empowerment, but when the hand of the lama touches the head of the patient, of any person, since the lama is always in meditation and has a realization of his true being, then just by physical contact a great number of diseases and harmful external influences are cleared. There is some difference between placing one hand during the time of the blessing, and placing with both hands. In our ordinary bodies, we have five main organs and six hollow organs. When we are talking about lama then we can talk about five special or miraculous powers and six special powers. The word is *siddhi*. The touch makes contact with all the *siddhis*.

After the medicine is prepared, then the best way would be if the doctor does a certain ceremony of consecration of this medicine in connection with the Buddha of Medicine. If the doctor does not have time then it is customary to have a monastery or whole congregation of monks do that consecration; or, if that is not possible, then by inviting a lama for doing it over the medicine. Basically the medicine, because it is already blessed by Buddha, will have the power to cure the diseases, but by doing this extra consecration on the medicine then it will not only have that power of curing the disease but will also protect the body of the patient from harmful influences that can also shorten his or her life.

Because most of you do not know how to read Tibetan, then it is very difficult to apply all these different ceremonies and do it properly. It is also difficult for the Tibetan medical system to become widespread because there are very few Tibetan doctors. I will talk about how, with a way of thinking, with an attitude in yourself, how you can also derive benefits from this system. It begins with the Buddha of Medicine we have seen on many *thangka* paintings.

His color is blue like the sky. Since our bodies have been formed basically through ignorance, our being has the three poisons of passion, aggression, and stupidity or dullness. By meditating on the Buddha of Medicine, by concentrating on the flow of nectar, and by certain visualization techniques like envisioning nectar being thrown over oneself or the radiation of light, then the power to cleanse all beings of these influences can manifest. The Buddha of Medicine has centers of body, speech, and mind. From the center of body, speech, and mind we visualize light rays that come from each of these centers. At the center of the body which lies in the forehead, the embodiments of enlightened body, is the letter OM. If we do not know this we just think of white light emitting. It enters the head, dissolves, and then comes down until it completely pervades the whole of the body. By the action of this white light, the reaction of our system, our body, is in the *rlung* or vital energy. This vital energy travels throughout every channel of the body. Every pathway is a path for this *rlung* to move around. So, this white light will act on this *rlung* which is going down when we are cleansing the body downwards with the white rays. Then we will have the feeling that all of these diseases are coming out of the body in the form of black fluids. They melt into the ground and then we think that we have been cleansed of all the diseases caused by *rlung*.

Which are the diseases, in this case, that will be pacified, which have their origin in *rlung*? The first one is *srog rlung*, which as a disease manifests a bit like craziness. The second one is trembling. The third one is that the mind is unhappy, a kind of depression. The fourth one is sudden anger or hatred that also makes the mind unhappy. All of these are visualized as coming out in the form of black liquids and leaving the body. We wait for a minute to have confidence that we have been cleansed of all this through the power of the white rays. Then we go and receive the blessings of the speech of the Buddha of Medicine.

The center of speech is in the throat, and the embodiment of the power of speech is the red letter AH. We visualize this light which is mainly red but also contains the other main colors. This penetrates through our throat and after entering our body it fills up the whole body with this light. This red light will appease diseases of the liver, of the lungs, of wherever the blood circulates in the five organs and the six hollow organs, also diseases connected with *bad-kan* or phlegm, in which one does not have strength because the body cannot derive basic nutrients. So, all these are cleansed, and when they leave the body we feel that we have been cleansed from all diseases in this category.

Then, we will see the blessings of mind of the Buddha of Medicine. The embodiment of the mind of the Buddhas is in the heart and it is in the form of the letter HUM. From the letter HUM innumerable light rays come, mostly of the blue color, but they also contain the other five colors. They enter our body through the heart and then, once inside, they fill up the body completely. In this way all the wrongdoings in that connection leave our body n the form of blue liquid and they enter the earth and dissolve in the earth. We feel that we have been completely cleansed. The diseases that are cleansed by these rays are diseases of the gall bladder. That means our flesh becomes more flexible because of the proper functioning of the gall bladder. Another function of this is that our mind, our awareness, becomes more clear. Another result is that we are able to transform food into strong basic nutrients. All this we feel we have become blessed with.

These are the three letters: in the forehead, OM, in the throat, red letter AH, and in the heart, a blue HUM. OM AH HUM. So you think about these three letters and light rays proceeding from these letters. Also, you can visualize these letters in your ordinary, Western style of writing. If one this regularly, following the practice of what we discussed yesterday about cleansing with the nine breaths, and continues with this short practice they will be protected from being sick. This is a way of protecting oneself from getting sick or contracting many kinds of diseases. There is no use of being apprehensive about getting sick. This is a method which is a very good means to prevent diseases from taking over one's body.

Regarding the different colors of light, absorption of this white light creates peace in the mind. One will have a good relationship with one's circle of family and friends. The red light that we absorb at the throat will bring about richness. Richness means progress in whatever one does. If one studies, then one's knowledge and intelligence will grow. If one is a businessperson, then whatever fortune one has will also grow. For instance, when we talk about the human body, we can look at the color of the blood. If the blood is perfectly red then the whole circulation is functioning well; the body can grow well and can be in a firm state. So, in more or less that same way, we can understand why relying on a certain color can bring about certain results. With the influence of the blue color, the person will be able to attract and to have power over whatever the person attracts. This is not done deliberately, it is not because he or she sets out to attract or control, but it just comes naturally.

So all that we have heard today is in connection with Buddhism and Medicine. And this is only a little bit!

10

Diagnosis in Practice

Now I would like to talk about diagnosis in the Tibetan system. I will diagnose the pulse of the person here, Lelah. One starts by examining the patient by his or her left arm. Then the doctor uses the right hand to measure the patient's pulse. One starts with the left arm because this creates the conditions for a quick recovery from the disease. It is more or less symbolic that the person is asking with the left hand "give me all the powers for my recovery." If one starts by the right arm, extending the right arm to the doctor, then recovery will take longer. However, this has to be done naturally, not deliberately. If one knows about this and then deliberately extends one's left arm to the doctor, one is doing this deliberately and it is not like a sign. When the person naturally, on meeting the doctor, extends the left arm then it is a sign that he or she will recover soon. If the patient enters the room where the doctor is with the left leg first then it is also a sign that recovery will be quick. This does not have any relationship with whether one is left-handed or right-handed.

So, Lelah is extending now her left arm and I am going to check with my right hand, the three fingers of the right hand. There is a specific place where the three fingers are placed on the arm of the patient. One takes as a reference the first wrinkle of the wrist when the wrist is bent. Counting from that first wrinkle down a distance equivalent to the size of half of the patient's thumb, one starts to place the fingers from the point downwards. A condition for the doctor to be able to read the pulse is that the doctor's hands should be soft and also they should be warm. If the hands of the doctor are cold then he or she will not be able to properly read the pulse of the patient.

Then, one places the three fingers; that is, the index, the middle and the ring finger. These fingers should be placed flat and then they should not be touching each other; they should be placed in the right way. The pressure that the three fingers apply on the arm is also different. The index will press to the level of the skin, the middle finger will press to the level of the flesh, and then the ring finger will press all the way down to the bone. This is because the shape of the arm is going from fat to thin towards the wrist and the index finger, which is placed closest to the wrist, is measuring only a little bit of flesh. The middle finger is measuring a bit more flesh, that is why it presses harder. Then, the last one, the ring finger, is on a part of the arm that is already quite thick so one has to apply more pressure than the other two.

The first pulse that is read is the constant or natural pulse of the individual. This can be of three kinds: male, female or nuetral pulse. At this point, the doctor has to concentrate without being distracted and read this pulse. Concentration has to be strong and away from the coarse mind. Coarse thought or perceptions are naturally not perceived because one is so concentrated in the reading of the pulse. Only subtle thought can be there.

Next I will check the constant or natural pulse of this individual, of Lelah. Generally speaking, you do not have anything bad, but you do have some kind of problem, which is not usually talked about in public. [Doctor Dolma asks if there is any problem discussing your disease. The volunteer replies that she doesn't mind.] There are three kinds of problems with you. You can eat well, but then when it reaches the stomach and in the process of digestion, the liver is not able to extract from the food the essence or the basic nutrients. Connected to the liver are the eyes, so you do not see well, you have weak eyes. When you stretched your arms and I looked at the tips of your hands, they were not very stable. This indicates that some *rlung* or vital energy has set into the kidneys. Because it has entered the kidneys, then you have some marks under the eyes and also from the waist downwards you do not have much strength. In the back of the neck you have this channel. There are two channels, two veins that go from the back to the gums. Their connection is with the upward moving *rlung* that I mentioned yesterday, the *rlung* that is also responsible for firmness of the body. Because this is a bit disturbed, your mind becomes unhappy easily. If this is not taken care of now, then you will have problems sleeping and this will become even worse if nothing is done. It is not so much that you are unhappy, but that you feel afraid very easily; at certain situations you very readily become afraid or nervous. Then you become apprehensive that this will happen or that will happen and you worry. In connection with your gums, your teeth are not very strong because the roots of the teeth in the gums cannot hold very strongly. These are the three main problems that you have.

There are many more small problems, but you have absolutely nothing to worry about. There is medicine, blessed by the Medicine Buddha, and you take that, please. As to diet, you should avoid sausages and food that is made from the insides of animals. Also, you should avoid sour food. For instance, if you are eating vegetables, then you usually use vinegar, soya sauce; these things you should avoid. Then in terms of behavior, you should not bathe in cold water. You cannot have black coffee, but you can mix it with milk.

[Dr. Dolma asks who would like to be examined next.]

When touching with the upper part of the index of the left hand, this reads the lungs. The lower part reads the large intestine. With the upper part of the middle finger, the doctor reads the liver and the lower part reads the gall bladder. With the upper part of the left ring finger, the doctor reads the functioning of the right kidney and the lower part of the urinary bladder.

Your constant pulse is feminine, the female pulse. That is a sign you will have long life; it is a good pulse. If a woman has a male pulse that is also a good sign. [Dr. Dolma asks Keith if it is alright to say these things.] Your body does not have any big problem, but also it is not free of problems. You have a kind of middling state of health. Your main problem is with the *rlung* which is called pervasive *rlung*. At this point you are young, so the harm of this disturbance is not great. When you are very interested in doing something, in doing some job, or carrying out some task or another, but then as you are concentrating very hard and the mind is fixed to do it, soon you start to sweat. And, after doing that particular job, you become very tired. You become tired one day, and the next day you feel strong, and the day after that you may again feel tired. You do not have constant firmness in the sense. Generally speaking, we would say that the body does not have much strength. Your liver is in a good state. The whole process of dispersing the blood is being carried out properly. You have a problem with the spleen. The function of the spleen is to purify the blood sent by the liver, so this function is not being done properly; it cannot cleanse the blood properly. On account of this, the natural warmth of the body does not function properly and your hands and feet become cold easily. When you eat food, and after digestion of food, there is gas in the stomach. It is not a gas that is coming out of you, but it stays in the stomach. These are light kinds of problems that you have now with your body; there is no great sickness. When we say that you have a female pulse, it does not mean that you are effeminate. It means that from the time of conception your pulse has been a female pulse; we consider in our tradition that when a man has a female pulse and a woman has a male pulse, this is a good sign.

Your main problem is in a disturbance caused by this pervading *rlung*, which stays in the heart. To take care of that, you should take a pill which is very aromatic. You should take only one pill a day for 30 days. The name of this pill is *sem-dhe*, which means 'happiness of mind'.

We have now shown the way of diagnosis with the pulse. And some people may have confidence in this method; others may feel it is a little bit too much. Anyhow, I have shown with these examples how we do it. Any questions?

Q. Which herbal or mineral combination is used for cancer patients?
A. For cancer in the large intestine, only herbal medicine is used; there is no other ingredient like jewel medicine or anything like that. You want to know which kind of herb? I can say in Tibetan, but the common name here would be difficult. In each flower that we are using, there are sometimes three degrees of color. For instance, there is a dark yellow, light yellow, and orange, also with white and any other colors. Sometimes there are five shades of colors, sometimes three, sometimes two, and so forth. When we talk about the flowers of herbal medicine, then it is very difficult for you to have an idea if we cannot show you. On the other hand, one example where you would have an idea is a pearl.

There are seven kinds of pearls that we use in medicine, seven difference between qualities of pearl. Although these seven categories of pearl are basically white, still there are different shades which divide them into these seven groups. Some of them are big and have a reddish kind of hue. Others are white, with some reddish hue that is paler. Some others are completely white. Some are white with a bluish brilliance or hue. Some of them are white with a yellowish kind of glare. And some other are like water. Some others have no color at all. Tomorrow we are bringing some medicines, some herbs, so may be we can show you some herbs then.

Q. Is there a different system of pulse diagnosis of a psychotic patient who is crazy or mad?
A. Any kind of diagnosis which is done by pulse is done in the same way, whether the patient is a crazy person, or if it is to see how a baby will be born. For disease or for anything else, it is like a telephone. A telephone is only one phone, and it uses one cable, but many kinds of messages can come through that particular source. In that same way, the doctor can read or hear the signs or messages that the different organs send through the pulse. And by reading these messages, the doctor can know if it is a problem of the lungs or of the liver, or some other problem. Everything can be known by reading the messages of the pulse.

Q. In the West we say that there is a physical material in the body which makes a person psychotic.
A. We examine mainly the pulse, but also we look at the body of the person because also there are many bodily signs that this disease manifests. We will look at the eyes, we will look at the expression of the person and the way he or she speaks, and at many different aspects of that body which will tell about the disease, even if it is a mental disease.

Q. Are psychotic people able to be cured by Tibetan medicine?
A. There are many types of psychosis in the Tibetan system. The medicine used is moxa, and there is also massage with a certain medicinal substance.

Q. What about this treatment of curing psychotics by placing them in different colored rooms?
A. Any kind of disease arises from the three humors of *rlung*, *mkhris-pa* and *bad-kan*. For instance, *mkhris-pa* is connected with heat and then *rlung* and *bad-kan* are connected with cold. When a person is put in a specific room with a certain color, then it can relieve him or her temporarily. It is like a good connection for his or her relief, but it is not a cure from the root; it has not eliminated the disease.

Q. Can cancer be viewed as a curable disease?
A. When we deal with cancer, it depends on how advanced that disease is in that person. There are four degrees that have been laid out. We can cure the first and the second degree in 100 percent of the cases. This has become already well-known in India. The third and fourth cases are cases that come to Tibetan medicine after having undergone a very drastic treatment under other types of medicine. For instance, people who have been operated on, or people who have had chemotherapy or so forth. In these cases, the success is then only 60 or 70 percent. For this particular disease one uses mostly precious medicines; that is, medicines made from precious substances. Together with these precious substances, then one uses herbal medicines or leaves, or flowers, and so forth. And then we put them all together into one type of medicine. In the case where there is already an inflammation or swelling, we apply moxa.

11

Child Conception

Today, we will first talk about the conception of a child in the womb. Secondly, we will talk about the birth. And thirdly, we will talk about examining the child and determining whether the child will live or die, the general health of the child, etc. For this child or being to take conception in the womb of the mother, three conditions have to come together. If these three conditions are not present then conception cannot take place. For the sperm coming from the father to impregnate the ovum in the womb, there are two possibilities: that it can conceive and that it cannot. There are three conditions for the sperm to be considered healthy: the color should be white, it should be heavy in weight, and also when a drop of this sperm is touched it should have the ability to stretch between the fingers. When these three conditions are there, then the power of the sperm is considered strong. This semen has by nature the subtle energies of the five elements. This semen then is able to procreate; it has that kind of power. It is a living organism.

Now we will consider the ovum coming from the mother. It also has to be free from three kinds of defects. The correct ovum comes when the menstrual blood of the mother does not stick in cloth and can be washed properly, that means that it is clean. The second condition is that it should have the color of the blood of a rabbit, light red. This means that it should be intensely red. When the menstrual blood is not healthy then it has a yellowish color or brownish color. Healthy menstrual blood is completely red and it is uniform in its color. It does not form different patches.

In this way, we have seen two conditions for conception, a healthy sperm and a healthy ovum. Still, even after these two units, if there is no consciousness in the intermediate state called the *bardo*, between death and the next birth, then conception cannot take place. These are the three conditions for conception to take place. The consciousness of the being, the sperm, and the ovum. If the merit of this consciousness in the *bardo*, the intermediate state, goes in accordance with the ovum of the mother and the sperm of the father, and if there is a coincidence between the merit of the consciousness and the other two characteristics, then conception takes place. Otherwise, it does not.

We will explain what is meant when we say the 'merit' of the consciousness being in accordance with the other two characteristics or not being in accordance. If the mother, who is about to conceive the child, is for instance wealthy and from a good family, then the consciousness that is in the *bardo* state, who is going to unite with the mother, should also have the merit to deserve the kind of position that he or she is going to be born into. That is what is meant by 'merit' and the coincidence of the necessary factors. When that consciousness in the *bardo* does not have the right 'merit' to connect with the father and mother, (for instance, in a previous life he or she has not been generous enough or collected enough merit by his or her actions and so forth,) then the merit is not in accordance with the position of the man and woman now in intercourse. Even though the consciousness of the being may leave the intermediate state of *bardo* and enter the conjunction of ovum and sperm, it will not be able to hold to that; there would be a miscarriage or even an abortion. That is only because the merit is not connected with the circumstance of the parents. When this being does have good merit and has performed good actions in the previous life for its own karma, and the parents have a situation that is not very fortunate, then the two kinds of merit coincide with each other and conception can take place. There will be no defect in the conception itself.

For the consciousness to leave the *bardo* state and enter the womb for conception, there are four ways of entering the womb. This first case that we will examine is that of ordinary beings, ordinary people like us, people who do not have realization. A being who has the ordinary type of consciousness cannot choose rebirth, the conditions of rebirth, or the future parents. He or she would be, like us, groping in darkness and unable to recognize the difference between a good birth and a bad birth because there is no light on at all. In the same way, that being does not have any perception of the different states that it could choose, of the different parents it could choose, but in this case it takes parents without any control over the process. Without knowing and without remembering anything, it enters the womb. And also at the time of birth it does not know who are the parents or what are the conditions at that moment. In that state of darkness, the child is born.

The second type of being is one who has accumulated a great deal of merit through good activity. He or she is a kind of universal emperor, or otherwise a being who, through their realization, is called a stream enterer in the Buddhist tradition. This is a being who has a certain degree of realization and has entered the stream of those who will soon be freed from rebirth. This is one stage of realization, stream enterer.

So, these second kinds of beings, when they enter the womb, they do it with awareness of the process and can select the place, time and family of birth. However, these being, after being born, mostly lose the consciousness or remembrance of what they were before entering the womb of the mother.

The third class of being is that of the Bodhisattva. That means, a being who is intent on obtaining enlightenment for the benefit of other beings. There are ten spiritual levels of Bodhisattvas. We are now considering the Bodhisattva of the first spiritual level. He or she also can select his parents.

This being can choose from many types of parents of different circumstances. It can choose parents who are practitioners of the dharma. When this being does so, he or she enters the womb with clear awareness of the whole process, after choosing precisely the parents he or she wants to be reborn with. After the birth, the child will not have the clarity to say who he or she was in a previous life, but it will have strong imprints from the previous existence and will be able to—although not clearly—have these strong impressions in his or her mind about the previous life.

The last kind of being that we will consider is Boddhisattvas of highest realization. They are Boddhisattvas who are abiding in the purest spiritual level of the eighth, ninth and tenth Buddhist stages. This has been done in old times and also is being done now-a-days by great lamas who can select their rebirth.

It was also done by Lord Buddha who, before taking birth in this world, was in the Tushita heaven and was already a being with such a level of realization. So, before taking birth in this world, he examined many types of visions to see who would be his parents. He chose the Queen, Mahamaya, considering the caste, the qualities of the person and many other characteristics. In order to come into this world and to determine a path for other beings to become liberated from existence, he took a deliberate rebirth. Before coming down, he made Maitreya the regent in Tushita Heaven, he who will be the next Buddha. And after that, he entered his mother, not as an ordinary being does but through the crown of the head. In a similar way great lamas now-a-days take deliberate rebirth. This is later recognized as reincarnation or *Tulku*. However, the only one who can enter through the crown of the head is an extremely realized being like Lord Buddha. All of these beings, having entered the womb at the moment of conception, will be completely aware of the process. After birth they will remember who they were, who their parents are, and so forth, because they have chosen the whole thing. In the case of Lord Buddha he was not born in the usual way, but was born out of the right side of Queen Mahamaya while she was holding onto a branch of a tree with her arm. Although these pure beings are also born from the womb, all the suffering of having spent all this time in the womb is quickly and easily cleared. That is another type of characteristic of a realized being taking birth.

Now we will talk about the ordinary type of birth by ordinary beings. The emotions that take the consciousness from the intermediate state into the next womb are passion, aversion, and also an element of jealousy. If a being is destined to be a boy, then when he sees from the intermediate state his prospective parents in intercourse, then he will have aversion towards the father and attraction towards the mother. These two emotions are also present in the second and third level of beings that we just talked about, but it is the degree of intensity that varies—they have a lighter emotion, but still they have the emotion. Although this consciousness in the *bardo* does not have a real form, a real body, still when it leaves the *bardo*, in his perception of his body that does not really exist as concrete, he will show his back to the father and his front to the mother.

This process is reversed in the case that the consciousness is going to be a girl. It will feel aversion toward the mother and passion or attraction towards the father. In the perception of her illusory body, she will give her back to the mother, and her front to the father.

There is a difference if this couple is accustomed to having intercourse and experiencing bliss. The quality of this bliss is higher when the actual conception takes place than the one experienced usually. They will feel very happy, and also the bliss will be much more intense than at other occasions. Then after that, they will feel really satisfied. The woman will lie down and feel more tired, her body will feel more languid and relaxed. They will both know that it has been a very special occasion, but they will not know specifically that conception has taken place.

In this conjunction of the consciousness of this being in the *bardo* with the sperm of the father and the ovum of the mother, the influence of the subtle energies of the five elements is present. The five elements are earth, water, fire, air and space. We will talk later about what effects each of these elements has in the process of child conception.

We will talk now about their influence on the sperm and the ovum. Three characteristics or elements in the body of the newly born baby come from the father. They are the bones and the bone structure, the spinal chord, the seminal vessels and semen. What comes from the mother? The three main things that come from the mother are the flesh, blood, and skin. What comes from the consciousness itself is the consciousness and the five organs. That is, the ears, eyes, nose, tongue and the sense organ of contact. All of these come together with the consciousness from the intermediate state. All these different contributions from these spheres—the father, the mother, and the consciousness—completely merge with each at the time of conception.

The subtle energies of the five elements of the father and the five elements of the mother then start to function and create an effect in this whole process. The influence or effect of the subtle energy of the element of earth is to create in this embryo the foundation of solidity, of hardness or firmness. When we are making dry or solid status the earth element is the one that patronizes it very firmly. In this embryo, whatever is moist, whatever liquid there should be in the body, these are all a function of the subtle energy of the element of water. It is as if, in the making of a statue, we are mixing clay with water. If we just want to make a statue with that ground clay, that powdered clay, it will never take form. So when we mix it properly with water, then we can make any form we want.

For the embryo to grow, to ripen, it needs warmth. This warmth is provided by the element of fire. If this element of fire were not present in the process, it would be like leaving a piece of flesh out. Flesh already has the element of earth and of water, but alone it would just go bad, it would rot. So, in the same way, for the flesh in the body to grow solidly it needs the element of fire. For example, when we have built a statue of clay, if we do not cook it in an oven with the element of fire to make it hard, then it can be destroyed; it is not something that can endure. This happens with the embryo.

The function of the energy of the element of air is to provide this body that is now formed with flesh, blood and the rest, with circulation for making it light, and most of all, for the breathing ability of the foetus. If that element of air is not present or not functioning properly in the embryo, it will die in the womb.

The last element is the element of space. The child, that foetus, needs space to grow. If that space is not present, for instance if the uterus is too small to accommodate the growth of that foetus, then at some point the foetus will be choked. The element of space has also to be there to accommodate that growth. The element of space is also necessary in the process of growth and creation. Going back to the example of the statue, if we want to take the statue and put in a box that is too small, perhaps an arm or an ear of the statue would be broken and so forth. The same is the case with the child.

The conjunction of the three characteristics merging with

each other in the womb does not mean that at this very moment the navel of the child is formed. The point where the two ovaries meet in the uterus of the woman—this point would be in conjunction with the navel of the baby. The reason why, after conception, the menstrual period is interrupted is because the menstrual blood usually goes through these two ovaries in the menstrual cycle. When there is no conception it goes through these two channels, the ovaries, and then it leaves the body. During conception, at this point where two ovaries meet there is a child, and therefore the blood goes to feed the child; the blood does not go out.

At this time the mother should eat very substantial food. It is very important that the mother observes a good diet because the child is going to form its navel, and the whole growth derives from that. Regarding the diet, she should procure food that has the six kinds of tastes. From the time of conception until the actual birth takes place, there are 38 weeks that will pass.

We will now start with what happens with the first week after conception, and which *rlung* or vital energy takes effect at that point. The names of the *rlung* will be given in Tibetan. It is probably better than in translation. The basic, fundamental *rlung* of them all will be now explained. There are many kinds of *rlung*. The basic, the most fundamental energy of them all is called the *nyon-mongs chen-gyi yid srog-rlung ah rnam-pa chen* (the vital energy of deluded mind and life force in the syllable of letter AH). It is the energy that sets the mental activity into action. This energy will be moving and will make the letter AH in the womb, just like when we see an airplane in the sky sometimes with advertising letters in its smoke. In the same way, the air will be moving and making with movements the form of the Tibetan letter AH. This letter is the highest of them all, the supreme letter. Whatever one does, whether practicing a certain type of meditation, or doing the breathing meditation of yoga, this letter has a specific and very important place in the whole system. Before any other letter was formed in the world, the first one that existed was the letter AH. Likewise, before the five elements take form, after conception, in this new body this air in the form of letter AH is there. The function of the *rlung*, when the *rlung* is drawing this type of letter, is to mix and to completely amalgamate the subtle energies of the five elements of the mother in the ovum, and the five subtle energies of the five elements of the father in the sperm. This consciousness also has the subtle energies of the five elements as well. So, all these five elements from the three spheres are completely amalgamated by the action of this *rlung*. It is as if this *rlung* is stirring these elements together to completely amalgate them.

rLung is immaterial. We cannot see it. Yet when we want to blow a fire so that it becomes stronger, we blow it with a bellows and we cannot see the air, but still the fire grows; it is more or less like that. Something that we cannot see, but it has a function, it works.

So then, after this complete stirring or amalgamation takes place then the first form that this embryo starts to take is a bit circular. It looks a bit like yoghurt. At that moment, the mother's belly will be big.

In the second week, another air, *prana*, starts to work. This *prana* is called *rlung kun-du sdud-pa* (the all encompassing vital energy).

The action of this second *rlung* is to give more solidity to that embryo that is being formed. That embryo, as we mentioned before, had looked like yoghurt and could not take any form, it was too liquid. So, by the action of this second *rlung*, it becomes more solid and it has now the consistency to take form. Now, it would be more like cheese. Cheese, though it has a certain hardness and consistency, is still flexible, it is still soft.

In the third week, the third *rlung* comes into action, called *mdzod-kha* (the treasury vital energy). By the action of this *rlung*, the embryo becomes even more solid than before. It would be more like old cheese, that kind of solidity, and consciousness is achieved. It is still soft, but is more solid.

In the fourth week, it becomes even harder, or more solid, than before. And the mother's womb, which becomes big until this time, again recedes and becomes thinner. It is the same *rlung* as before, but it is working more intensely now. There are two functions of that *rlung*. For example, I am a lecturer and I can talk sometimes about gynecology, and another time I can give a talk on *prana*; it is the same. The same person is talking but there are two different subjects. Also at that point, the belly of the mother will be protruding at the center and will become depressed at each side. This is because the form of that embryo is elongated and is vertical in the uterus.

In the fifth week, still the same *rlung* functions. By the action of this *rlung*, it becomes even more rigid or harder than it was before. The embryo has more firmness, like a piece of wood, for instance. It does not bend so much as before. At that point the power of gender exists in the baby, but still the sexual organ has not been formed. However, the power or the energy of possessing a certain sexual organ is there. At this point, this level or phase is called "the hardness is now changing" because this is the moment in which all the channels and all the veins will be formed and all the different airs in the organism will be formed.

These are the three main *rlung* that are responsible for the formation of the body. And, from then on, each week there will be new elements formed, like new channels, new veins, and also different kinds of *rlung* are created.

The first part of a body that is formed in the embryo is the navel. From the navel, the three main channels are formed. These three main channels are the channel of life, the channel of air, and the channel of strength.

What goes in the channel of life is the foundation of the universal consciousness, the basic foundation consciousness. It will be comfortable there, I hope! During the seventh week this central channel grows upwards and, 16 finger-breadths of the child upwards from the navel, the heart is formed. Then, at the level of the heart, a center of channels is formed which is called the *dharmachakra* or the wheel of Dharma. This coincides with the eight vertebrae in the back.

It continues to grow upwards, and when it reaches 14 finger-breadths of the child upward, it is at the throat. It forms the throat, or what will be throat. The throat then coincides with or is at the same level as the first vertebra. At the throat, a center of channels is formed which is called the wheel of enjoyment.

And then it grows upwards until it reaches what would be the crown of the head. At that point it forms another wheel of channels, which is called the wheel of great bliss. When this wheel has been formed, the five sense organs take slight form. We can see them, but they are not yet very clearly formed, not very definite. At the beginning there is not much differentiation between the body and the head, when we are talking about the seventh week.

Between the seventh and the eighth week, all these different organs in the face and head become more differentiated, as compared to the body. That means, the head becomes more like a head by the seventh week. By the eighth week, these organs become even more clearly defined.

During the ninth and tenth week, we can discern the upper part of the body from the lower part of the body. They already become differentiated but still the limbs have not come out. Then during the ninth week, the shoulders are formed. They become pronounced, and also the hips are formed. So the bones of the shoulders and the hips already take their characteristic form. At that point that embryo, that foetus, looks like a fish.

In the eleventh week, the holes are in the organs and they start to form clearly.

In the twelfth week, the five organs start to form. The first one is the heart. The second one is the lungs. Third is the liver. Fourth is spleen. The fifth one is the left and right kidney.

Then, in the thirteenth week, the six hollow organs start to form: the stomach, the small intestine, the large intestine, the gall bladder, the uterus, and the urinary bladder. If it is a boy, then instead of the uterus, it would be the seminal vessels.

In the fourteenth week, first the legs develop and then the arms. Although the body now has a form as a human body, still it is not completely differentiated in its fingers and so forth. The limbs are just coming out.

During the fifteenth week, the limbs take their final form. All the different fingers and the toes are formed. In the sixteenth week, the nails in the fingers and the toes are formed.

In the seventeenth week, all the veins and nerves that connect the organs inside the body, and also the ones that we can see that are the closest to the surface of the body are formed. From all these visible and invisible channels, that means veins and nerves, all kinds of ramifications of veins, channels nerves and so forth grow. Up to this point, the foetus does not have a consciousness of its body; the concept of its body is not yet formed. At this point another type of *rlung* which is called *te-gong gi rlung* starts its function. And that is the starting point for the child to begin to experience its body. The action of this *rlung* is that, through its influence, a vein is formed connecting the stomach with the liver through which the basic nutrients of the food can be assimilated by the liver. Then, the spleen and all the vessels for the purification of the blood are formed. At that point, the face, because of the shape of the foetus, is called tortoise-face. It looks like a tortoise.

Then in the eighteenth week, already the life has been formed. At that point, a rlung which is called *srong-gi rlung dri-ma med-pa* (the stainless vital energy of life force) starts its action. It is a *rlung* which is absolutely pure, without any type of contamination.

Around that time, the mother observes a certain diet so that she can give a beautiful appearance to that child. She should avoid or reduce intake of hot spices that make the mouth hot, like chillies and black pepper, and food that creates heat. Of the cold types of food, she should avoid buttermilk and whey. At that time, if one stops eating artificial colored food, or artificial kinds of food, then that is also good. This is observed at this time in the formation of the child because most of the flesh and the fat of the body are formed. Many babies, when they are born, have skin that looks a bit like snake skin or like fish. The reason for this defect in the skin is that the mother has not observed a right diet at that point.

In the nineteenth week, the *rlung* that starts to function is called *shin-tu phra-ba'i rlung* (extremely subtle vital energy). This means that it is immaterial, it is not evident. The result of the action of this *rlung* is that all of the different pathways and the tendons are formed at this point. This *rlung* not only creates these required pathways, but also imbues all these different parts of the body with the ability to function in their respective capabilities; for example, to move the tongue to create saliva, and so forth.

Now, in the twentieth week, the *rlung* which is called *shin-tu brten-pai rlung* or extremely stable (or firm) energy starts to work. Through the action of this rLung the whole body takes the firmness of a body because it works on the bones, which up until this point have been flexible but not hard. At this point, the bones become hard, the whole structure becomes defined and firm. Inside the bones, the marrow starts to form. At that point, four classification of bones starts to be formed. The first classification is long bones: thigh bones, the femur and the long bones in the arm. After that the bones that form are the flat kind of bones. These are the ribs.

The shapes of these were there before, but they were not defined specifically as certain bones and they were not firm. It is like when we burn, for instance, a piece of paper on which something has been written. We burn it in fire. Then, the burned paper will be there and we can also see the letters written. If we want to preserve it, it is not possible because there is no firmness or solidity in the paper. In the same way, that kind of design is already there, like where the ribs are and what the ribs are, but they do not have any strength or firmness. Now the firmness is given to these bones. The third classification of the bones that are formed at this moment are the round bones. This means, for instance, the bones of the joint. These different bones have this rounded part. The fourth classification is bones that have such a round shape that they could even float, like the skull, the shoulder blades, and the kneecap. These are big and they are hollow.

Then, in the twenty-first week, the rLung which starts to work is called yang-dag par bskyed-pai rLung (The Perfectly Generated Vital Energy). Most of the elements of the body have been formed in this foetus, like the bones, different veins and nerves, and so on have been-formed, but the flesh and the skin still needs to be formed even more. What has been formed in the skin up until now is the inner-skin of the different parts, but the outer skin is only formed in the twenty-first week.

In the twenty-second week a wind that is called *kun-du rgyal ba'i rlung* (invincible vital energy) starts to work. Through its action, the different channels will begin to act. The blood will begin to circulate, water will circulate, and menstrual blood will come to the female. All of these different pathways grow; they expand to wherever they need to go. At this point, then, the sense organs like the eyes become finally defined. That means that we can see already the different parts of the eyes like the eyeballs, the coloring, the iris, and so forth.

Then in the twenty-third week, the *yongs-su dag-par 'dzin-pa'i rlung* (the vital energy of complete grasping) starts to function. Through the action of this energy of *rlung*, all the hairs start to grow, the bodily hair and the hair on the head. All of the pores begin to give rise to hair. Also, the nails become hard; until then, they were flexible and soft. At that point, the mother will have acidity in the stomach and also heart burn. This is not a sickness, it is just a result of the growth of the foetus at this stage. If the mother then is diagnosed that she has some disease of *bad-kan* and if she is given some medicine to warm up her body on account of that diagnosis, then that would be very bad for the child, because the growth of hair will be impaired in that child.

In the twenty-fourth week, the *rlung* working at that time is called *rlung kun-du'phya-ba* (the ever-moving vital energy.) At this time the foetus will already experience feelings in relationship to all its inner organs. How does this manifest? If, for instance, the mother jumps very heavily, then the foetus feels this kind of feeling of fear in its heart. Or if the mother lays on her belly, or presses the belly too hard at the sides, then also the foetus will experience a localized pain at certain organs. At this point it starts to feel and to have to connect through feeling with all his organs. In order that the foetus does not have an injury or problem with the liver and eyesight, then the mother should observe certain rules of conduct. At that point, she should abstain from any intoxicants like wine, beer, or hard liquor. The second kind of diet rule she should observe is that she should abstain from rich, greasy food, and also from food that brings about obscurations, like pork and food that is made from the inside of an animal, like sausages.

In the twenty-fifth week, the *rlung* that starts to work is called *grong-khyer 'dzin-pa'i rlung* (vital energy within the city bounds). With the action of this *rlung*, the child will be able to breathe through the nose. At that time, the mother should observe her way of lying down. She should not lie down on her belly, for then the child's nose and mouth might be pressed. She should not also lie down forward. If she rests on her knees and then lies down forward, the child's six senses will become impaired. If one bends the leg like this, pressing the stomach, then the child's arms will experience that pressing and may break, or it may cover its own mouth or nose.

In the twenty-sixth week, a *rlung* that is called *skye-ba sngon-mar grub-pa'i rlung* (remembrance of previous lives energy) starts to act. At that point, the child's awareness become very clear and can see his or her former lives. The child can see if he or she was a pure being or an ordinary being, what type of birth he or she had before this birth.

From the twenty-seventh to the thirtieth week, gradually all the different sense organs, which are already functioning, develop further. The color of the body becomes more developed. In these four weeks, there are three kinds of rlung present: *sman-yon rlung, rlung me-tog phreng-ba, rlung lcag gi sgo* (*sman-yon* vital energy; flower garland vital energy, iron gate vital energy) that work is unison. Through the action of these three *rlung* working together, the ability of all the channels of the body, veins, nerves, etc. becomes more developed. Especially the five main veins in the heart develop. As I said before, there was one central vein and four other main veins or arteries around it in the heart. As a consequence of the action of one of these *rlung*, the child can move a bit and be able to move its body, to stretch its arms, legs, and so on.

The child is connected to the placenta of the mother, and derives the nutrients through the placenta to its navel. Then, the child begins to experience the sensation of eating. I have forgotten one thing. The child also eats. When it is eating, the child is taking nutrients through the placenta, but experiences or imagines that it is coming through the mouth. The child moves its mouth as if eating something, and eats dirt from the environment. At the point, it is important for the mother to avoid exertion with the body and to observe regular times for sleep. She must also avoid eating non-nutritious food. If one does observe this kind of behavior, then there is an early birth at that point because these conditions are not met. The child would be born premature.

Then, from the thirtieth up until the thirty-fifth week, another *rlung* called *rlung me-tog sdud-pa* starts to work. At that time, the child and the mother will not coincide in their states. Sometimes the mother is healthy and the child is unhealthy, or if the child is healthy, the mother might feel unhealthy. They will experience this dissimilarity between each other. At that point the child has already grown to its full extent.

When we consider the face according to the shape of the child, the first face was tortoise, and at this point the child looks like a pig and has the face of a pig. This is the thirty-fifth week. It just looks like a small piglet. This is just an example, the child is not really a pig.

During the thirty-sixth week, then the child starts to experience the dirty environment which exists in the mother's womb. At that point in the mind of the child, five types of perceptions arise which cause the child to wish to be born, to leave that environment. These wishes to leave the environment come from the perception of uncleanliness, foul smell, experience of darkness or a feeling of being imprisoned and a feeling of uncomfortableness which the child does not like. The fifth one is that the child's mind is unhappy. When these five perceptions, known as *mngon-sar mi-dga-wa-te skyo-wai 'du-she-nga*, these five feelings exist at that point, then the child wants to leave that environment. The child expresses this feeling to leave the womb by moving a lot; his or her arms move, the whole body starts to move in the womb. At that point, the mother should visit the doctor regularly for examination.

There are three types of positions in which the baby can be positioned in the uterus. The proper way of position of foetus in the body is when the heart is inverted or upside-down. The second one is when the body was formed with the head upwards. This is not the right way, but it is also not the wrong way; it is kind of like a middle way, but at that point she will need help from the doctor or from the midwife to correct the position. The third position, which is improper or wrong, is when the child is horizontal. If this is the case, there is a great deal of danger for the mother, especially for the child. The doctor then should put the mother in the hospital and then through gently moving the position, through gentle touch, the doctor should move the position of the child's body to the correct position. This movement can be corrected, and has to be corrected by the thirty-seventh week.

In the thirty-eighth week, a *rlung* that is called *thogs-me' rkyen* (primordial causal energy) starts to work. The function of this *rlung* is to somersault the position of the child so that it comes head first.

At the time of birth, the mother will experience three types of pain. At the beginning, she will experience pain only in front. The second type of pain is not only in the front, but is also in the back. The third one is when the water is expelled; before the child comes, water is expelled. These three degrees of pain go in accordance with the way the cervix expands. In the first type of pain, it just only opens, the bones that form the cervix region come apart a little bit. Then, the second type of pain, they come apart more. And the third type, then they come apart to the greatest extent; at that point the child can come out through the cervix.

The child will come out together with blood, and with serum, and many types of impure fluids. In the Tibetan style of giving birth, the mother would be on her knees. As soon as the child's head comes out, then the doctor should clean the child's nose from the blood that comes also together with the birth, the menstrual blood. If the doctor does not clean that, then it will create problem later.

After the head comes out, then in a few minutes the whole body, together with all of the impure stuff, will come out. After the child comes out, the umbilical cord will be presented in different ways. Sometimes the umbilical cord will be around the neck, and sometimes it will be just loose. If the umbilical cord is coiled around the neck, this is a sign that the child is a pure being or that the child has great merit. In the second case, when the child and the mother are separated by a long length of umbilical cord, then this indicates that the child is of a peaceful, good nature. If the umbilical cord is too short, then this indicates that the child will have the characteristics of being proud and very short-tempered.

We have now seen the process of birth of the child. Now we will see how the umbilical cord is cut. After the child is born, the doctor should pull out the remaining umbilical chord. The placenta has still not yet come out, so the doctor should pull the umbilical cord three times. Each time the doctor will say a prayer. The first time the doctor will pray, "May this child be healthy," the second time, "May the child live long," and the third time he or she pulls, the doctor will say, "May the child be happy."

The doctor will have to now tie this umbilical cord with a string. The first knot, which is closest to the navel, the doctor will tie counter-clockwise and make a knot. The second he or she will tie a bit further from the navel, and then he or she will tie it clockwise and make a knot like that. From a four-breadths distance from the navel, the doctor will tie another knot. This is to prevent the loss of blood that would go into the placenta. Right after this knot, the doctor will cut.

After cutting the umbilical cord of the child, we then take care of the mother. So that she does not have any problems of *rlung*, we cover her for a minute with a thin cloth, and then we feed the mother with warm butter and also soup made from fat and bones.

The child, after delivery, will cry. So we take the child and we turn it around so that it is lying on its belly. Some traditions then indicate to hold the child upside down by its feet at this point. This is not a proper way of handling the child because up until this time the child has very soft and weak internal organs. By putting him or her in that position, it can be harmful. In our tradition we take the child as we said before lying on its belly, and lift up the lower part of the body so that his or her head is a little bit lower. Then we clean the child's nose of all the mucous, three times. Then, the doctor, who will have cleaned his or her hands properly, cleans the insides of the mouth of the child. Three times, the doctor will kind of sweep down the tongue. Then we wash the child with water that is neither too hot nor too cold, just warm. Also, this water will have saffron in it.

According to the year in which the child is born, there will be a particular element that characterizes the child. Each year it changes. Suppose the child's internal element is the element of wood. The internal element of wood is connected to the external element of earth, so the color collected with that is yellow. After the child is washed, then we should wrap him in a cloth which corresponds to that element, in this case yellow. This is like creating conditions of auspiciousness.

After this, we will let the child sleep. We will lie the child on its back, not on the belly, in a place where there is not direct, strong sunlight.

In order to create the conditions for the child to have clear intelligence, great intelligence, and to have stable intelligence, we make a powder mixture of three kinds of medicines. Drawing this with the medicine, we make the design of the letter HRIH. We touch this and put a tiny bit of this in the child's mouth, on the tongue.

This same medicine, made of three ingredients, we put in melted butter and with that paste that is formed we will touch first the navel of the baby, then the throat of the baby, and then on the crown of the baby's head. We will take a little of this paste and then slowly massage the area. This is done so that the baby's three basic conflicting emotions of passion, aggression, and dullness, may be appeased, creating a condition.

The next step is to give the child three drops of clarified butter from the hands of a lady. The lady has to have three characteristics: her father and mother must both be alive and she must have children. She puts three drops in the mouth of the child in order to create auspiciousness for future of the baby. Also, the child has to be washed the next day in the same way. It has to be done like this for a week, washing the child once each day.

When washing the baby, the chest should be held by the left hand of the mother. First we wash the legs, and the body with soap, and then we rinse the soap away. Then we should proceed up the head, and only wash it at the end. The reason for going in this order is because it is always more uncomfortable for the child to have his or her head washed, especially if some soap gets in the eyes. When the child cries very strongly, it could still harm the navel. So, if we started from the head, since we still have to bathe the rest of the body, it would be a long time for the baby to be crying. If we finish with the head, still if the baby cries there is less time left in the process of bathing, and the baby will soon be taken away from the bath.

The child will mostly be breast-fed, but after one month we would also give rice powder and also roasted barley flour to the child. These would be mixed with a teaspoon of melted butter and given to the child, but mostly he or she is fed on his mother's milk.

Also, the child has to be massaged every day with warm butter. The butter is applied around the navel and massaged there, but mostly it is the legs and the arms that are massaged. Some children have legs that become crooked later when they stand up. This massage is done so that the child's legs are straight.

Most of the time, during the first three months, the child should be left lying down. The child should not be kept erect because this will create problems in the liver and other internal organs. The child is kept lying down for three months. If the child is kept erect, the liver may fall from its own place a bit. This would not happen if the child were kept in a lying down position.

After three months, we can start giving the child more coarse kinds of food. This coarse food should be given at a regular time, but this does not hold true for breast-feeding. Breast-feeding should not be at fixed intervals, but should be given whenever the child wants.

We now go back to the mother, whom we have kept for a whole minute covered with a thin cloth. After one minute, we have to start doing something to get the placenta out. For that purpose, we give a certain medicine. After three minutes, as a result of the action of this medicine, the placenta will come out. Some women have a very large placenta. If this is the case, the doctor will wash his or her hands and will use something to take it out. The doctor does not need to insert his or her hands into the cervix. After washing his or her hands, the doctor will tie the remaining umbilical chord to two fingers and will give two turns around; with the left hand the doctor will then start to pull slowly. With the right hand, the doctor will push slowly at the placenta. So, in this way, the placenta will come out.

This placenta should not face the open sky; it should not be seen by a dog or by a human. As soon as it comes out, it should be put into a pot with the lid closed. Then the astrological calendar must be consulted to find the most influential direction for that time of the year. Consulting the calendar, we should choose a place to hide the placenta inside the earth. If at that time the calendar says that the east is more prominent, then we should hide the placenta in the western direction, in the ground. In our belief the placenta is considered a very impure thing. If it is left open for the sky to see it then certain deities who protect places, like earth protectors and other kinds of deities and beings, would get upset by seeing something so impure. Because they get so upset, then they could create some sort of bad influence in the child that would manifest in the form of skin diseases and other kinds of problems. Because of that, we dispose of the placenta in the most inconspicuous way. We just hide it and even the sun is not allowed to have contact with it.

The mother has to be washed clean. After washing her we should give a massage to the mother using warm oil, especially on the back at the level of the waist because all the bones and joints have been strained. They have to be aided by warm massage to help with the recovery of the mother. In the Western tradition, and also in the Indian way of dealing with birth nowadays, usually they sew the vagina of the mother. However, in the Tibetan tradition, we do not do any stitching. Just by the strength of the massage, adequate food and care, then it will again join by itself, naturally.

The first step in breast-feeding and how to start breast-feeding is to massage the breasts very properly, because the first drops of milk, which has a yellowish color, must be disposed of. This cannot be fed to the child. Also, there is a problem with the mother if she starts to just directly give the yellowish milk, the impure milk, because the pores and the cells that feed the child this milk would become damaged. From this, many cases of breast cancer develop. The way to do is to massage the breasts properly, and extract all the yellow milk until it becomes white. When the milk is white, then that is the right milk to feed the child. On the side of the child, if it drinks that yellowish milk, then he or she will have problems of digestion and it will also harm the child's stomach.

Before starting to feed the child, then the mother should first press her breast; with the milk that comes, she should sprinkle and then wash the eyes of the child. This will cause the child to have good eyesight. This should be done every time the baby is to be fed.

In some births, not only the child comes out and placenta comes out, but also the uterus in some cases comes out. This has to be treated by the doctor. The uterus which has come out should be washed with the same type of warm water as we said before. Before putting it back in, the doctor wash his or her hands and nails properly. The whole process is to wash the uterus, and then to put it inside. The doctor should anoint her hands with a kind of medicine that will prevent infection. The doctor's left hand will go inside the uterus and he or she will push it until it is in the right place. The uterus should be warmed up through the water. If the uterus is put back at a cold temperature, that brings complications. After this operation has been done, then the mother will not be allowed to stand up for a whole week, she must lie down always with the legs a little bit higher than the body and the head a little lower. She should not sit down. Whenever she has to walk, for any reason, then she should walk with short steps. And also she should not climb upstairs. In this whole process there is one rule of behavior that should be observed, which is very important. There are actually many, but if one observes this particular one, then it will prevent the woman from becoming sick with female kinds of diseases.

For a month after the birth of the child, the mother should not have sexual intercourse. If this happens then she will have problems with her back. She will have problems with discharges, and also she will have a problem with her menstrual cycle.

In our tradition, after three days the lama will do a purification ceremony done with burning juniper leaves, with aromatic smell and smoke. Usually, after three days we will give a name to the child, after this ceremony has taken place or during this ceremony.

Also in our tradition, once a month we will make sweets with saffron, and other very delicious kinds of candy. Then we will give this to any child who comes to the house. This will be done up until the child is nine months of age.

In this way, the child reaches one year of age. At that point, according to our tradition, we will take the child to a lama who will cut a small portion of his or her hair and perform a ceremony for long life. The lama will then give a specific name to this child, which will be the name used during his or her life.

When I was born, my name was La Chenzin. After one year I was taken to this lama who gave me the name Lobsang Dolma. Generally speaking, the lama will usually give one of his names as a first name. As a second name, any other name is given. This is the reason why today, when one meets Tibetans, there are a great number with the same names like Lobsang, or Tenzin, or Thubten, and so forth. This is because lamas have given their own names as the first part of the name.

In this way, we have seen, very briefly, the whole process of conception, of growth, of birth, and of care for the baby and the mother.

Now I will continue discussing certain related subjects. Some children die in the womb, some children die in the moment of birth, and some children die after having taken a few steps. Let us consider the child that dies inside the womb. There are two reasons for this. First, the child who dies by natural conditions. These natural conditions are fixed by the child's own karma. And the child dies because he or she still has life from the former birth and is living the remaining few weeks or months in this mother's womb. If it is three months, then that is as long as the child is supposed to live. If it is five months, then five months. Then, naturally he or she will leave the body as a dead child, this is what is generally called miscarriage in the West. In Tibetan medicine, it is called *tse-lhag* or "living the leftover life".

The second type of death in the womb would not be by a natural miscarriage. It is caused by certain circumstances or conditions that happen to the mother; for instance, if she falls down, or eats something that is very improper, or has an accident or so forth. When these happen, then this creates a commotion in the system, and this causes the miscarriage by circumstances.

Let us now see the case of the child who is dead just as soon as it is born, or in the process of birth. There are also two cases. The first case is the case of the child who has bad karma through the actions of the previous life. In the womb, its position is horizontal, that means that he or she is in the most inconvenient position. Then the child's arm, when he or she is turned around, comes out. This is a problem when there is no doctor around, which is the case in most Tibetan households where birth is aided by a midwife and not by a doctor. In that case, the child would not be able to be taken out of the womb. It has to be understood that the child is dying because its lifespan is at an end.

The other case is when the child, with the aid of the doctor, is taken out of the womb. The child comes out of the mother, but as soon as he or she lies down the breath stops and the child dies. This is also considered death during the process of birth, because it is so close to the process of birth itself.

The other case we are going to see is of a crawling baby. After nine months of age, a baby usually starts crawling around. Babies who die at this stage of life, most of them die because their lifespan is up at this point; they are not supposed to live any longer. In these cases, the child dies because the natural lifespan is coming to an end. The child is destined to live for a certain amount of time because of past actions and karma. So, there is no way of reversing or changing that. The child will die in any case. There is nothing to be done about that; no medical treatment that can extend his or her life.

So we have talked about children and the deaths connected to their lifespan. Now we have completed this subject today.

Q. Is it possible to have intercourse during pregnancy?
A. Usually, in the Tibetan tradition, we say that one can have sexual intercourse up until the eighth month of pregnancy. However, from

the eighth up till the ninth month, the child is moving already, he or she has more control over the body, so it would harm the baby to have sexual intercourse. If the parents of the child are so passionate that they still want to have intercourse, then they should do it in such a way that the belly is not pressed down. Intercourse should be had keeping in mind that the woman is pregnant. If, in the process of intercourse, one gets carried away and forgets that there is a child in there, then both partners might do something which is not good for the child. It might end up in something very harmful for the child and the mother; one should keep this in mind.

Q. If the mother wants to have an abortion, is that in the karma of the child?

A. Yes, as we said before, it is another case of children who die in the womb; they can also die by special circumstances which, in this case, is that the mother wants to abort it. However, it depends because the child did not have a life span; it means that the lifespan of the child was in coincidence with that. Most important is the child's karma. The child's lifetime is not extended, and the mother coincides with that and decides to create a condition or circumstance that will eliminate the child.

Q. Is the decision of the mother to have an abortion predestined by the karma of the child?

A. There is a great connection between the karma of the child and the decision that the mother takes. However, the mother should also think very, very clearly beforehand what she wants to do. If she does not want children, the best means is that she should avoid them through contraception or through some other way of prevention.

If the mother decides to get rid of the child once the child is conceived, then during the first two months after conception, the child does not experience pain. After that time, when the navel has been formed and all the five elements and the channels and everything has already been formed, then it inflicts great pain on the child to abort it. After two months, there will also be bad consequences for the mother's health, because the child is already being fed and everything; all her elements and her structure also will be harmed by this decision.

Q. Could you say something about the karmic effect of abortion?
A. The karmic effect of abortion is very bad. The mother decides to have the abortion only once. It is only on one child. Yet, the consequences of this action, as it will reflect on her own future, is that for many lifetimes she will have to be the one who is aborted by someone else. Everybody became very surprised at what I just said. I tend to think that many of you are in that position.

After what I have just said, there is no reason for any of you to be afraid, because there are many ways of purifying this. Now I will talk a little bit about this.

In ancient times, there was a person who was instructed by his guru to kill one hundred men and then to make a rosary with the thumbs of each of the victims. He was told that was the way that would lead him to salvation. This person had already killed 99 persons and he had their thumbs around his neck, and then he was looking for his next victim. The next victim that he chose was his mother as there was no one else. His mother at that time was visited by Lord Buddha, who was asking for alms or food. When Lord Buddha knew that this was going to happen, he said, "Don't kill your mother, kill me because I have ten thumbs." He showed his hands...he manifested many hands and then ten thumbs for the rosary. Then this man, he is called Anguli Mala, became very happy because he thought, well, then I do not have to kill my mother. Then, he decided to cut the thumbs from Lord Buddha's hands, but then he could not cut it. He became very irritated because he could not cut the thumbs of Lord Buddha, and he threw away his sword and began to fight and argue with Lord Buddha.

Then Buddha started to talk very gently to this man. Buddha told Anguli Mala that if one's motivation is pure then whatever path of progress that is made will also be pure. If one's motivation is bad then whatever progress is made will also be impure. So, you should also look upon your motivation. Then the Buddha told him about the ten wrongdoings and the ten virtuous actions, teaching him on positive kinds of behavior. Then he told him, now you have created a great deal of bad karma because you have killed 99 men, but still if you practice, if you clear this bad karma in this lifetime, then in this life you will become a saint, an *arhat*. Then this man started to take teachings from Lord Buddha, and through his actions he cleared this bad karma, and at the end of his life he became an *arhat*. Similarly, there are ways in Buddhism to cleanse wrongdoings like abortion, etc.

12
Massage

Today I am going to talk about massage or, in Tibetan, *sanye*. *San* means vein (i.e. energy channel or blood passage) and *ye* means to massage. Doing this treatment improves the flow of blood and vital energies. For the sick, it is used to relieve pain and in times of health it is used to help maintain a state of well-being. There are thousands of points on which to give massage, but today I will talk about the most useful and frequently used points.

1. Giddiness:
There are two major points for massage to be applied. From the eyebrow's center, one measures three *tsun* (length from the tip of the patient's thumb to the base) upwards. The massage is then applied with three fingers. Then from the back of the neck you measure four fingers up. At the forehead point, massage with three fingers back and forth (vertical) and the back point, massage sideways (horizontal). This is just for general giddiness caused by weakness. It gives energy. When the person is young, you can give the massage quite strongly, and when the person is old, it must be given delicately.

2. Headaches:

Headache have two main causes. First I will speak about headaches caused by bile. Everyone of us has three veins around the eyes. It is here where the wrinkle comes when we get older. For a hot type headache the doctor should massage from the back. This point is found one *tsun* from the tip of the ear. Mostly use the middle finger, and with the other two fingers just press. Two fingers press while the middle finger massages back and forth. It is important to use your fingers in a different way depending on the location of the veins. According to their location, you have to use your fingers. The point is at the center where the three veins meet. If we check carefully there is always a pulse beating. This is one place to check how serious it is. It is also quite important to know before giving acupressure whether the headache is caused by heat or cold. If it is caused by heat than give a dry massage. If it is caused by cold then it is connected with energy or *rlung* problems, which are the second cause of headaches. This massage is given with a little oil or butter. Add to it a little nutmeg, then it is like magic. Magic massage. Just massage until all the oil disappears. The *tsun* measurement is from the front of the ear, one *tsun*.

3. Half headache:

At the back of the head, there is a crevice. If the patient has a headache in the left side of the head, use your left thumb or finger. If it is a right-sided headache, use your right thumb or finger.

4. Half or full headaches caused by sinus problems:

The symptoms of this are yawning, tears coming from eyes, dripping nose, etc. The point is at the base of the skull. Use the thumb or three fingers.

5. Blockage in hearing due to sinus problems:

The symptoms are that there is sound inside, like buzzing, and it is difficult to distinguish other people's speech. Use two fingers on either side of the ear. Using the two fingers you automatically reach the point. It is at the base of the ear near the delicate bone.

6. Hiccups:
There are two little bones near the jugular vein or aorta. The life energy is passing through this so moxa or acupressure can not be used. These would upset the life energy. So massage should be given to the side of this. Use only the index finger, gently and smoothly. This will stop hiccups. Do it in a circular motion or half-moon motion.

7. Energetic wind causing heart problems:
This air, wind or energy corresponds to air pressure pushing water up a system. In the same way, this air or energy is circulating in the whole body. It pushes the blood, and it blocks the blood. If the nature of the energetic wind is not working properly in the heart, there is fast breathing, palpitations and sometimes a dull pain in the heart. To find the point of massage, count four ribs down from first rib. On the fourth rib are located the massage points of major heart veins. Give massage there with four fingers for about two minutes—one minute with the palm, then with the four fingers, then palm, etc.—until relief is felt.

8. Sharp pains in the heart:
Massage between the breast in the center of the chest. When giving the massage, the hands must be warm. A cold hand cannot give the massage. To find the point, take a string from one tip of the breast to the other; the center of the string is the point. When giving the massage, keep the breasts warm with the other hand.

9. Imbalance of digestion due to liver ailment:
The liver point is on the right side, about the position of the tip of the elbow when the third finger is touching the ear tip. The symptoms of liver weakness are severe pains in the liver. Here you massage with your right hand and four fingers. Using the left

hand, you can find the spleen point in the same way. The spleen point is massaged if there is pain in the spleen or if there is nausea. You can find these two points either standing or sitting, as long as the spine is erect.

10. Pain in the stomach caused by worms:

There are two parts; the first is to relieve the pain, the second is to push out the worms. The symptoms are pain, sweating and cramps. This means the pain is caused by worms. Most of the worms grow in the stomach because this is the storage place of food. To find the point of massage, use four fingers. From that point measure down one *tsun*. This is for relief of pain. Expelling Worms: A pillow should be placed under the back. When you find the point, you have to massage down. When doing this massage the worms come out of the anus. Usually the person knows he or she had worms by the stool. If worms can be diagnosed by the pulse, then that is best. The pulse feels undulant and flat. In addition to detecting detecting a pulse of the flat type, the person can check by themselves in their stool. Usually our body is full of worms. Many worms help to give energy to the body, but others cause disease. These worms should be taken out. This idea of worm includes bacteria. This massage is performed by using four fingers to push downwards.

11. Ovary massage:

This includes problems with menstruation. In the West many women who may have a defect in the ovaries undergo surgery and their ovaries are cut. This is very dangerous because there is no way to ever conceive a baby after this. Massage helps, and there is no need for surgery. To find the point, the patient should be standing up. Touch the pubic bone and measure one span up. The massage should not be deep; rather it should be surface massage. The best time to give this massage is at the time of menstruation. It helps for the menstruation to be normal. It cures problems of the ovaries and gives energy to conceive a baby. The massage is done a little like squeezing something. When the patient feels like urinating then that is enough massage. If you continue past this point, urine will just come automatically.

13

Breathing Exercises

There are two ways to do breathing exercises. One is safe, the other can cause problems.

In Tibetan yoga, the breathing exercise to clean the energy channels and blood passages called *tsa-rlung*. *Tsa* means channel or veins, and *rlung* means air or vital energy.

To do breathing exercises properly there must be an object. Just to breathe without thinking of any object is called empty breathing. If a person has heart or *rlung* problems then this is further increased by empty breathing. You should think that by your breathing exercise you are purifying either the organs or the blood. If you do just empty breathing then this just shortens the life span.

In the Tibetan system, it is said that a person should take a certain number of breaths per day. Every human being should breathe this number within 24 hours. There should optimally be 21,600 inhalations and exhalations. The number should be balanced. When we do very fast or slow breathing, the number is not balanced. The breath should always be normal. The normal breath is the natural breath.

Since our bodies began to form, two types of breath have been connected: the natural breath and the long-life breath. The natural breath goes out and does not return. The long-life breath goes out but does return. If you breathe very fast then the long-life breath cannot return. The natural breath blocks the long-life breath. Due to this, the length of your life decreases.

There is one breathing exercise which prevents or cures diseases caused by imbalance of the three humors. Or, if there is no disease, then this exercise is good for maintaining the balance of the three humors. This exercise is good for maintaining the balance and preventing imbalance of the three humors. Certain diseases can also be purified with this breathing exercise.

The posture for the exercise is as follows. Sit cross-legged in the vajra position with the left hand under the right hand, with both being held in the lap. One's back is to be kept straight, with the thumbs near the navel. Relax into that position. As you relax, concentrate your mind. If you don't control your mind, your mind just goes out roaming. This doesn't help.

The fourth finger closes the right nostril and you start to breathe naturally through the left nostril. Concentrate on energy coming up through the hips, navel, chest and throat. Energy comes out of the left nostril. This energy is dirty, black, and impure energy connected with desire (as one of the three poisons). So it is based in the hips and comes up from that area through the channels. Then when you have exhaled the black, impure energy, change the visualization as you inhale. Inhale the energy of the five elements collected together into one essence. It is whitish and clean. As you inhale this essence it goes through the left nostril, throat, heart and goes to wherever the vital energy is located in the body. The energy always passes through the left side channel. The right side is blood circulation channel. Do the same breathing and visualization three times. If you can visualize from the throat to the heart, from the heart to the navel, and the navel to the hips, that is good. Each humor has a different breathing exercise. Exhale first, to purify one's body of illness, then inhale, taking in the pure essence of all the five elements.

Next, hold the left nostril. This purifies bile diseases. The location of bile is on the right side, below the liver. Think that from the gall bladder a dark reddish yellow color mixed with energy comes up through the navel, the throat and finally the right nostril, to be breathed out. Always visualize that these energies are dissolving into the earth and not into the air. Inhaling the same as before, taking the collected essence of the five elements, white and clear in through the right nostril, through the throat, through the heart, through the navel and in to the bile point, the gall bladder. To find the gall bladder, touch the tip of your ear with your middle finger; the point where the elbow tip reaches indicates the position of the gall bladder.

Now hold both hands on your lap, right over left, with thumbs touching the navel. The next of the three positions is related to ignorance and the disease is phlegm. The location is in the brain. Ignorance means knowing nothing, darkness. The color of this energy is white and black mixed, sort of smoky grey. Think that this is the dirty energy of weak memory, depression, headaches, too much thinking, tension, etc. All this is visualized as grey energy. This energy pass through the center of the forehead through a small hole between the nostrils. If surgery is done on the nose you can see a small hole there. Actually, energy is invisible so you have to visualize this.

Suppose the person has an eye ailment, cataracts or weak eyesight, then the energy is taken from the weak eyes down through the center of the nostril. It passes out and into the earth. Then inhale as before taking in the energies of the five elements. These come up through the center of the nose. They come to the brain or to wherever you want them to go. At the same time you rejoice that you have received all these energies into your brain.

This clears the mind, cures depression and so forth. Just think that it is all cleared.

In the first exercise, to remove the impurities associated with desire you should also visualize a black bird also passing into the ground. Both the energy and the bird. The second one is for desires associated with aversion. Think that is mixed with a snake, and that both of these pass into the earth. The third one, ignorance, is associated with the dog, a fat pig with dog's eyes. This also passes into the earth with that energy. So there are nine different ways to do the breathing exercises.

If the person can do these exercises in the proper way it can definitely cure diseases. In many cases when the doctor cannot cure by medical means alone, for example eye cataracts, this exercise can cure the patient. Generally, for all the organs you can meditate on, take in what you need and exhale what you don't.

Q. Would breathing exercises be a benefit to people with arthritis?
A. Yes, it helps. When you exhale you take the impurity from the feet up.

Q. You have said that non-directed breathing exercises shorten your life. I have been doing this for 8 months to get strong and I have been wasting away, no flesh, no muscle, just skin and bones.
A. Dr. Dolma thinks that you did empty breathing exercises, because flesh or muscle grows out of the blood. So due to empty breathing exercise, your body cannot grow flesh or muscle. All the things you have been doing are for a fat person to get thin.

Q. Are there any special herbs for arthritis?
A. Yes, many good ones; single herbs do not help. They should be combined. Generally, arthritis medicine is a combination of 19 substances or ingredients. This can help for all different kinds of arthritis.

Q. Can you get it here in Australia?
A. Yes, you can get many in Australia. They are not very rare substances.

Q. What does empty breathing cause?
A. It makes the heart have palpitations, then you cannot get sound sleep, you yawn very often and get back pains.

Q. What effect does empty breathing have on the blood?
A. The nature of air is so cold and the nature of blood is hot. So the blood that flows from the heart should be hot. If it is cold, then it doesn't produce more blood. When a person is always cold in their hands and feet, it means they are not getting enough blood circulation.

Q. Are there any herbs you can use in a bath for general ailment treatment, like a mineral bath?
A. There are many. In the topic of minor surgery, it includes medicinal bath, moxa, acupuncture, medicine, massage, and leaves. However, it takes about a year to discuss all these aspects.

Q. Could you give some simple example of a medicinal bath?
A. You should know that for diseases like rheumatism and arthritis, medicinal bath is good. Like the Chinese say, ginseng is very useful. For us, we also use medicinal baths combined with other herbs. Five roots are combined to make the medicinal bath. It includes ginseng, and four others also. This is good for joint pains. For those who cannot walk, who have swelling of knees, or cannot stretch, if a medicinal bath is taken over one month then it can be cured. These five roots cannot be used in the natural way. They should be crushed, boiled or cooked, then kept for one or two days in a tight cover. Fermentation takes place. Then mix with water and use as a medicinal bath. This relieves pain and you get good sleep and become happy.

14

The Spleen and its Functions

Today we will talk briefly about the spleen and its functions. The spleen has four main functions:

1. Purifying the blood
2. Helping to mix the food in the digestion system
3. Clearing the body so there is a brightness to the skin
4. Lubricating all the liquids of our body.

If there is a spleen disfunction, then the nails, tongue and mouth become dry. Even if you apply cream, the mouth and nails remain dry. Also if there is a spleen disfunction many spots appear on the face and in the whites of the eyes, a bit like a rash. Another symptom is a noisy sound in the stomach. The stool that is passed is full of mucus and the person become increasingly weak.

The color of the spots in the eyes are a mixture of purple and black, and are located in the whites of the eyes. They should not be confused with the dark-yellowish spots caused by a liver defect. It doesn't matter whether the spot comes out in the eyes or on the skin. Some even come out on the tongue. The only thing you have to clarify is whether it is caused by the spleen or the liver. This is determined by the color. Also a liver weakness causes the person to become thinner and thinner, whereas with a spleen weakness the person remains the same in weight but becomes weaker and loses inner energies.

Q. My question is, what effect do different foods have on the organs? In Chinese medicine we learn that there are five different tastes. I am wondering whether you have the same five tastes and what organs they are related to?

A. Yes, in Tibetan medicine there is also this theory. In the medical texts related to diet treatment—food and diet—tastes are included. Each different taste affects different organs. Every food has a different categories of sweetness. For example, there is honey, sugar, raw sugar, black sugar; these are all sweet, but we have to clarify each different sweet taste. The different tastes of sweet give a different essence of energy to the body in the organs. So one kind of sweet is given for hot nature disease, another for cold nature of disease and yet another for combined hot cold diseases. For example, raw sugar is good for the blood, bile and fever. The organ it affects is the liver and production of bile. It gives energy to the liver and bile. So this is one type of sweet. Honey is good for bile and fluid, and also good to reduce weight. Actually, using honey one way can increase weight; using it another way decreases weight. Honey also gives energy to the brain and helps the spleen and skin.

Q. How do you use honey for losing weight?

A. First you have to boil one glass of water. Then when one third of the water has steamed away, put in one teaspoon of honey and stir until it is white, thoroughly mix the honey and water. When it becomes lukewarm, you drink it slowly in one complete go. You drink this before eating anything early in the morning. Before taking food in the morning all the nerves and veins are open and the honey circulates easily. It stops or blocks the accumulation of fat. This is for the person to get slim. For the person who wants to get fat, boil some milk and stir in the honey and drink. In losing weight there are many methods, this is describing just one method. Also you should not eat for half an hour after drinking the honey and water. So now we have talked about two sweets, raw sugar and honey. Honey is good for the combined hot and cold diseases. Now, brown sugar is good for cold disease and *rlung* problems. Brown sugar has two types, so for the medicines we usually use the whitish color of brown sugar. You take this for *rlung* problems and cold disease. It is not good for hot diseases or fever. it helps the stomach and kidneys, with digestion power and kidney power. According to Tibetan medicinal tradition, this should not be taken by itself because it's too strong. You must mix it with porridge, tea or butter.

This is just a brief explanation of food taste and how it is used in Tibetan medicine. All these five different tastes give energy to different organs. Sweet, bitter, pungent, salty and sour. Tastes in different combinations are also used medicinally, as combinations of taste affect organs differently.

Food combinations are also important. Taking certain kinds of food together make poison in our digestive system. For example, if you eat fish just after drinking cold milk then it turns into poison in the stomach and you lose digestion power. As another example, beer and yoghurt are not good. Together, they produce a poison in the digestive system. Also banana, yoghurt and pears eaten together make poison. Banana and yoghurt together or pears and yoghurt together is okay. The nature of the two fruits are different, one hot and the other cold.

Q. What tastes are good for the liver and spleen?
A. For the liver and spleen, two tastes combined are good: sweet and sour. Sweet tasting foods are good for the liver and sour ones are good for the spleen. Bitter tastes are good for the gall bladder (bile). Also, combined tastes of bitter and very sour is good for the gall bladder and for jaundice. Astringent or pungent tastes are good for the kidney. Salty tastes are good for the stomach and large intestines. Nutmeg-like tastes are good for the heart. For the lungs, carrot tastes, not sweet and not sour, are good. In Tibetan medicine, the color of food is not important.

Q. I would like to know about Tibetan herbal contraceptive techniques. While in India I heard very conflicting stories about Tibetan contraception. Some said one has to take the herbs for weeks together without thinking of men or sex and this can have a contraceptive effect for a year or two. Then others said Tibetans don't use anything, they have too many children—look.

A. I myself prepared a contraceptive pill, out of herbal ingredients, by combining eleven ingredients. Other Tibetans say that to use contraceptive pills is a non-virtuous action or sin. So it is not good to take them. Some people are superstitious in this way. They say that by taking the pill one is blocking off the birth of human being, so they don't take it. However, many Indian and Western girls and women are taking the pills, which have proved very effective for them. They are taking so much that there is always a shortage. Some girls have been taking it for five years, some for three years. Some write to me and receive it through the mail. There are no side effects. One only has to take the pills each day for seven days, then it will last for one year. This is an exceptional case for the Tibetans who think it is not good to use contraception. However, now many Tibetans are realizing that there is a population explosion, and many of them are using this method.

Q. How successful is it? Always or most of the time?
A. If the girl strictly follows the instructions, then it is very effective. If the girl cannot follow the instructions properly, then after four or five months she can conceive a baby. This depends on the user. They are simple instructions. On the fourth day after menstruation begins, the woman takes the pill for one week continuously in the morning. Then for 12 days, no sexual contact or sexual activities.

Q. No sexual thought?
A. If there is sexual thought or something like that, energy is pulled by thought.

Q. Are there any foods that you shouldn't eat while taking this pills?
A. Diet should be normal but you cannot use any other medicine while taking these herbal pills.

Q. A couple of questions before you get too far away from diet: In regard to craving a taste, if a person wants food with certain taste, like sweet or sour, is that an indication of natural craving? Is that a philosophy of Tibetan medicine?

A. Yes.

Q. The other question regarding taste: if there is a taste in the mouth and it is not a craving, but it is like a bitter taste or salty taste in the mouth, what is that an indication of?

A. If it is natural, without taking food and still there is some sweet taste for bitter taste—in the case of a bitter taste, this means that the gall bladder is over producing, there is an increase of bile.

Q. How could one correct that?

A. If this happens then you should avoid taking hot-natured foods, rich foods like butter, peanut butter, meat, etc. If you do this, the bile will come down. If you have a bitter taste and still you take the rich, hot-natured foods, then you will get jaundice. If in summer you feel fever and continue to take rich foods, you will get other diseases.

Q. How can fasting be used?

A. Fasting is good for two problems. The first is indigestion and belching. The second is when you always feel full after eating. The first is a phlegm problem; phlegm is up. For phlegm and indigested food, fasting is good. You should not go to sleep when fasting. It doesn't help. You should fast, then work. If you fast and then sleep, the problems increase. It is best to fast just on water. It is okay to drink tea, up until noon. After noon, you should not drink anything.

Q. What happen if one gets very very thirsty?

A. Just prepare some water with lemon, rinse your mouth and then spit it out.

Q. What foods are good for phlegm problems?

A. For phlegm, one should eat bread, vegetables, tomatos, cheese and yoghurt. If you have some sort of phlegm problem, fish, pork and oily food are not good.

Q. What should be done after a person has had hepatitis?

A. When a person has hepatitis he or she should rest in a place that is neither too hot or too cold, and not in open air. For diet, lemon juice is good, and also yoghurt without cream. Bread and rice are good, as are boiled vegetables without oil or too many spices. There are very good medicines for hepatitis. The principal medicines has eight ingredients and can cure hepatitis in one or two days. In Australia there are also many herbs to cure hepatitis but they are not being used.

Q. I was wondering what colors are related to each organ in Tibetan medicine, and if the same colors related to the chakras?
A. The heart is associated with fire, and the color is red. Lungs are associated with iron, so their color is grey. If the lung color changes to black there is a lung disease or lung cancer. Liver is associated with wood so its color is green. Spleen is associated with earth so its color is yellow. Kidney is associated with water so its color is blue, light blue. Five elements, five organs and five colors.

Q. Do you use tongue diagnosis and complexion diagnosis in Tibetan medicine?
A. Yes, complexion as well as individual organs—mouth, eyes, nose, speech and tongue are all used in diagnosis.

Q. Is there any relation between the five elements and the five chakras?
A. There is a different way of explaining the relationship between the elements and chakras in medicine and Dharma.

Q. Some Western physicians claim that they can treat the chakras by color and sound because some illnesses originate from the spiritual body. They use all seven different chakras. They usually associate certain colors to either activate or do the opposite. The chakras, according to this system, can be either stimulated or calmed depending on the color used.
A. Chakra healing is taught in the oral transmission not the text books. The physician should have practiced well, gone into retreat, performed meditation, etc. Otherwise, it doesn't help, there is no energy.

Q. They use the principle that a certain frequency is associated with each chakra. They have a machine that vibrates light and they set it at the person's chakra. They claim a good success rate.

A. There are many methods to healing in the four fundamental medical tantras. From these we get many methods of treatment. It is said in the *Oral Transmission Tantra* that the doctor can give light, initiations and mantras. However, he or she mostly uses medicines. Only for ailments caused by evil spirits are these other methods used.

Q. Can Dr. Dolma talk a bit about the second body, the body outside the material body? Can surgery upset the vibrations of the second body? I have heard that they don't use surgery in Tibet because of that.

A. Tibetans do not use surgery. It is not good for organs and bodies. It is just for the temporary relief of the ailments, but the inner energies are lost. It is not good for the whole body. There is less chance of a conventional treatment thereafter because of the loss of energy. For example, some girls get ailments if the ovaries are removed. Afterwards they get married and then they want a child, but there is no chance to conceive. So surgery has caused a problem.

15

Tibetan Medical Concept of Insanity

According to Tibetan medicine, the causes of mental illness are: very strong concentration in the mind, heating of the body through strong exercises and then cooling off quickly, losing too much blood, crying too much and worrying unnecessarily over family problems, and just worrying much. These cause either one or two types of insanity. The third main mental illness is called sexual mental illness. So there are three types: hot mental illness, cold mental illness and sexual mental illness.

First we will look at hot mental illness. The symptoms are that the person cannot control himself or herself, is overacting, is fighting with people, breaking things and not behaving in a normal way with other people. The treatment of such cases should be rough at first to frighten the person down. Immerse him or her in very cold water, or hold the person down on the floor. Sometimes beating is useful, not enough to hurt the person but to give a sense of fright. As you do this you should give advice and implore the patient to stop. In this way, by giving the person some sort of shock, he or she may get the feeling that they should control themselves. This is the behavioral treatment. The medication administered is a combination of 25 different ingredients. After giving the medication, the doctor applies moxibustion, not acupuncture.

The points of moxibustion for curing insanity are as follows:

1. Center of the head (Tib.: Tsotsa):

To locate this point, stretch a string across the head from ear to ear and then from the tip of nose to the back of the head. Where the strings cross is the point.

Another way of measuring is to measure 5 *tsun* from the tip of the nose. Each *tsun* is different according to different patients. It is a measurement taken from the first point of the thumb to the tip of the fleshy part of the thumb, not to the end of the nail. It is measured from the patient's thumb, not the doctor's. So it is not a permanent, fixed measurement but varies according to the individual. In Tibetan they use a small stick of bamboo broken to the proper size.

It makes no difference which method you use to find this point but sometimes using the string is a little quicker.

2. Heart (Tib.: Henna):

This point is to be found by taking a thread and stretching it from one breast to the other, and then finding the midpoint by folding the string in half.

3. One tsun up from the heart point:

For hot mental illnesses, measure one *tsun* up from the heart point.

Giving moxibustion to these three points helps for hot mental illness. The size of the moxa to be given is equivalent to the size of the tip of the patient's little finger. As it burns, it burns right down and then just pops out by itself. It should be put directly on the skin.

For cold mental illnesses, first I will describe the symptoms. The patient keeps quiet, stays indoors in dark rooms, sobs a lot, can't sleep at night, talks to himself or herself, etc. When you see a patient like this, it is cold mental illness.

The medication consists of two different ingredients. The three points for moxibustion are as follows:

1. First spinal, between the 1st and 2nd vertebra
2. Fifth spinal, between the 5th and 6th vertebra
3. Sixth spinal, between-the 6th and 7th vertebra

One moxa is given to each of these three points.

For hot mental illnesses, the moxa is firstly given to the head center, then to the middle of the chest and then one up from the chest point. You must do it in this order, otherwise the patient will not get better. When you give the moxa on the top of the head you are blocking the energies from coming out. Suppose, when the patient cannot control the mind, this energy is blocked and returns to the heart. As for giving the moxa to cases of cold mental illness, first give moxa to the first vertebra. After one week give moxa to the fifth vertebra. After a further week, give another moxa to the sixth vertebra. You should not give moxa to all these points at the same time. Giving them together is very strong and very dangerous.

Q. What is the effect of giving moxa to these points?
A. Giving moxa to the first spinal for cold mental illness gives heat energy. The fifth vertebra is connected to the heart nerves, so the heart gets energy. It also gives energy to the bones. Whenever there is weakness in bones caused by *rlung* diseases weakening the bone marrow, giving moxa to this point helps. Giving moxa to the sixth vertebra is to balance the thinking powers. Bone marrow problems are that you feel that your bones are hollow, sore or aching, like you have been beaten or bones have been bashed.

The third main type of mental illness is sexual mental illness. First the symptoms of the male. The boy is always talking about girls, saying he is loved by many girls and they are chasing and catching him. For the female, it is similar. The girl uses some instrument for masturbating and the boy massages himself. The name for this in Tibetan is *tsunmo*.

The Tibetan name for the medicine to cure sexual mental illness is *tsenti*. It means pills "to make happiness". These pills are made from a combination of herbs and fruit. Also the sap which is collected from the base of the pine tree is mixed with other herbs and used. You take it from just above the root of the pine tree. This sap is used for the female mental ailment. Ten different herbs are used. For the male you use nine different ingredients. For both of these patients, moxibustion is used rather than acupuncture. To find the female point you measure four *tsun* below the navel. This is one point. Another *tsun* below this is a second point. This is the seat of the sexual powers and warmth. For the sale, measure six *tsun* below the naval then two *tsun* to the right and two *tsun* to the left, three points.

Q. How can we know what herbs to use?
A. If there were herbal preparation rooms in Australia I can show you or go to the mountains and show you, or perhaps you can bring along a book.

Q. Acupuncture doesn't work alone, you also need herbs?
A. Yes, one needs medicine. There are some sorts of energies that increase sexual powers, and these should be decreased by giving the medicine. Then giving acupuncture gives relief.

Q. Is it possible to give acupressure and not acupuncture?
A. Acupressure is good for tiredness and blockage of blood circulation, or nervousness and depression. It is also useful for infertility in females and impotency in males.

Q. For what other diseases can you use acupressure?
A. It is good for improving digestion, relieving pains due to worms and headache, and so on. It cannot completely cure. For that you

must have medicine. It is also good for hiccups, yawning and trembling due to fear.

Some men discharge semen without control at night or with urine. There are two veins under the testicles: one for semen and other for urine. So give acupressure there with oil or butter. For women, too, acupressure to stop discharge is to be applied at the point where the hips meet the back of the pelvis.

Q. What sort of discharge is this treatment for?
A. All forms. In the first stage, the discharge is white, in the second stage it is yellow and in the third stage it is brown with very bad smell. Acupressure is also good for tiredness of the eyes caused reading too much or watching too many television programs. The eyes discharge white stuff or a water-like substance. Then give acupressure at the sole of the foot, the middle part where it doesn't touch the ground. Another point is center of the neck. These two points will cure eye tiredness. It is auspicious to stop at the point of curing eyes today. May be Dr. Dolma has opened your eyes.

16

Theory of Diagnosis—Child and Adult

Today we will discuss diagnosis. Diagnosis in the Tibetan medical system consists of three types. The first one is questioning the patient with five types of questions. The second one is feeling the pulse of the patient through contact. And the third one is examining the urine by looking at it.

Let us start by the examination of the pulse. Examination of the pulse as it is done in the West and as it is done in the Tibetan medical system are not alike. And even in our system, the examination of the pulse of a child is different from the examination of an adult pulse.

Child Diagnosis

We will start now with examination of the pulse of a child. Three types of examination are done on a child. The first type of examination is when one examines the backs of the ears of the child. The second type is done on the way the child cries when he or she is in pain. Since the child that we are concerned with is not able to speak because he or she is too small, then we cannot ask if there is pain here or there in the body. So, the third type of examination is done on the milk of the breastfeeding mother. That milk is put in water and then observed.

We will now deal with the examination of the ears of the child. The child should be put up against the light, the sunlight, and the doctor should stand behind the child so that the doctor can see the back of the ears from the back, and the sunlight would be coming from the front. When seen like this, one will notice many different veins in the ears, but many of them are too subtle. What one observes mostly is three main veins which are like the roots of all the others.

When examining the right ear of the child, the topmost vein will indicate the condition of the lungs and of the large intestine. The middle vein indicates the condition of the liver and of the gall bladder. The last vein, the lowest vein, indicates the condition of the right kidney and of the urinary bladder.

Then we examine the left ear of the child. First, the topmost vein will indicate the condition of the heart and of the intestines. The middle vein indicates the condition of the spleen and of the stomach. The last or lowest vein indicates the condition of the left kidney and also the condition of the uterus if the child is a girl, or the seminal vessels if the child is a boy.

Now we will see how these six veins, three on each ear, will determine the condition or the disorder that the child has. What one observes in the vein is the color of the vein. Each of the five main internal organs and also the six hollow organs can have their condition examined in this way. Each of them has a specific color, which I will explain. Now remember that the veins on the right ear indicate the conditions of the organs situated on the right side of the body, and the veins on the left ear indicate the condition of the organs on the left side of the body.

When examining the blood of the vein, if the color is brown or dark it indicates that the child has fever. In most cases when there is fever, if we want to check where heat is in the body, then the organs that will usually be connected to this heat, this fever, are the heart and the liver, in most cases.

When the blood in the vein that indicates the condition of the gall bladder is not red but is turning to sort of a yellow color, then there is a problem of bile, or the gall bladder.

The first symptom of the child having a fever or a problem of fever because of the bile is that the fever will show itself in the forehead of the child. It will then take over to the whole body, but it starts on the forehead.

We are now dividing disease also in terms of hot and cold, problems of the heart or fever and problems of cold. For the problems in the blood or in the bile, the nature or essence of these diseases is heat, is fever.

The child will manifest a problem of cold when the blood in the vein that we are examining turns to a very pale yellow. When this yellow color has a lot of white and the yellow is not uniformly distributed, then we can conclude that this is a problem of cold. This manifest mostly in problems in the stomach, problems of digestion and also that the lower part of the body of the child feels cold.

When we observe the vein and see a light reddish color because the blood is there, or sometimes there is mostly this very pale yellow. That is the manifestation of the problems of cold. When the veins shows that the color of the blood is very light, more like white, with no element of yellow in the color, then this indicates a problem of phlegm. The manifestation of this problem is that the child, whenever he or she eats something, will vomit. And also, the stomach of the child will be swollen.

When the child has chicken pox this will manifest as redness; the veins will be red and also the ears will be reddish. When one checks the eyes, the whites of the eyes have red veins. That will show clearly in the eyes. If, at that point, the disease is identified as chicken pox immediately, then the child will be able to recover very quickly, maybe even without medicines, just by observing the right diet. If this is not identified so quickly, then the child will need treatment with medicine.

When the veins in both ears show a dark color, then this indicates that the child is under some kind of negative influence from the outside. In our medical system we consider also influences from what we might call spirits, or some other kinds of beings, that intend to harm the child. So, this is not a disease but some kind of negative spirit that intends to harm the child.

When the child has the condition in the ears where, when one looks through the light, no veins can be identified because they are so interlogged, then that indicates that the child's long-life vein has been weakened. The child's life is in danger.

For this case there is no medicine that can clear the situation, because it actually is not a disease. Instead, one should do a certain practice to extend life. This practice for extending the life of some other being is very easy to do in the West. One can go to a seafood place, where they have living animals that the fishermen have caught and one can buy maybe a hundred small animals, small fish, and take them and put them back into the sea. These fish were destined to be killed, but then their lives are saved by throwing them back into the sea. That would be the treatment in this case. This is the easiest way in the West.

In Tibetan culture we also resort to going to a lama for a special ceremony to extend the life of the child. Then he will do maybe a ceremony of Tara or another type of ceremony which is intended for clearing the obstacles for the child. Then also a long-life initiation or empowerment would be given to the child, and long-life pills also. So, we also resort to the aid of lamas.

Examining the Crying of the Child

We have now seen the examination of the veins of the child behind the ears. The second method of examining a child is by listening to the way a baby cries. The parents can also use this type of examination; it is not always necessary to consult a doctor for that.

When the child has a problem in the liver, then the way of crying changes. The usual tone of the crying will change. Between cries there will be longer intervals than usual. It will not just cry for a short, uninterrupted period. Also, the mother should examine the color of the eyes, because the eyes are connected with the liver. The color of the eyes will also have changed a bit.

When the child has a problem of cold, then his or her way of weeping or crying will be different from normal in the sense that it will be more full, more swollen. Every time the child cries it will be for a shorter period of time than in the case of the liver trouble.

When the child is under the influence of a malignant spirit it will cry in an irregular way. Sometimes one cry will be long and the next cry will be short; there will be no constant tone when the child cries.

Examining the Milk from the Mother's Breast
The third examination of the child is done by observing the breast-feeding of the mother. The milk of the mother should be poured in a wide container, four finger-breadths high. A cup should be placed on the table. The cup should be filled with water. The doctor will then take the milk from the mother, catching the milk in the wide, clean container with the help of clean implements, starting with the right breast. Then the doctor will pour the milk in the center of the cup filled with water. If the milk remains on top of the water and does not mix up to the bottom, then there are no worries for the child. The problem is just that the child does not digest the food properly and that it feels uncomfortable; because of this, the child cries. So, in this case, there is no reason to worry and there is no reason to take the child to the doctor. At such a situation, if one takes the child to the doctor thinking that the child has some problem, then the

doctor may give some medicine that will harm the child. It is not good to give medicine to a small baby.

From the left breast of the mother the doctor should take three pressings of milk in the prescribed container. The water in the cup has to be replaced with fresh water. When the milk poured into the water and it does not sink to the bottom but stays in the middle, then there is not much to worry about; still, the child has some problem and the doctor should be consulted. The doctor, after examining the child, will be able to tell exactly what disease the child has.

For the third examination, again fresh water has to be put in the container and now milk from both breasts should be poured into the water. If the milk stays on top or goes to the middle then, as seen before in the first case, there is no need for treatment. In the second case, the child should be taken to the doctor. However, if the milk sinks to the bottom, this indicates that the child will die. When the milk falls to the bottom like a solid column, then this indicates that the child has a very serious disease that might be possible to treat, and the child could recover. When the milk falls into the water like different clusters of milk and does not immediately spread, but remains like clouds, then this indicates that the child is under the influence of evil spirits. When, after leaving this cup with water and milk for half an hour, the color will change and we have to look at it against the sun. If the color of the water and the milk has become brown after half an hour, then this indicates that the child has a disease in their blood. If the mixture turns yellowish then this indicates a problem of bile. If the mixture of water and milk shows bubbles after half an hour, then this indicates that there is a problem of phlegm. When the mixture turns bluish then this indicates a problem of *rlung*. If after half an hour, in the water and milk mixture forms like frogs are seen, then this indicates that the local deity has been offended because one has not disposed of the placenta in a good way, which might result in some problem for the child.

Liver Treatment of Children

There is a specific treatment known for cases of weak liver, problems with the lungs, kidneys, and so forth. There are medicines and the illness can be treated. I will now explain more about the situation where the liver has fallen from its own place. When this happens, the child will not feel pain but will become thin. The child will usually not look upwards, and the head will always be bent down. The water in the child's mouth will dry up a bit. Sometimes the child will have diarrhea, sometimes the child will vomit. If these signs are there and one cannot go to a doctor, then the mother herself can correct this problem.

For this one should have a *melong* made with an alloy of three kinds of metal, the alloy of which is called *lee*. The mirror should be connected to a tassel and the mirror should have one hole, and the tassel is connected to this hole by a ring. The doctor coils the tassel in his or her hand and holds the mirror by this extension where the ring is put. The mirror then has to be cleaned properly. The child should lie down on its back on a hard bed. The problem with the liver is that it has fallen down a bit. The doctor first uses the mirror cold, as it is, and pushes it three times upwards. After doing this, the mirror should be polished with a cloth. The liver that has to be lifted should be held now by the left hand of the doctor, and then the doctor should do this circular movement three times, from from the right and moving upwards. One should continue pushing upwards and then the liver will be moved upwards and come to its own place again. Until that happens the mirror does not slide easily on the skin of the child, but will be interrupted on its path. Once the liver has reached it own place then the mirror will slide easily on the skin. For a few minutes after the liver has been placed in the right position, the mirror should be placed on the liver and it should then be tied up with a cloth. For this problem then we do not need medicine. This is the way of treating the case of a fallen liver. There are other similar ways which do not require medicines.

This is briefly the diagnosis of a children. Let us now start the diagnosis of adults.

Adult Diagnosis

The examination of the pulse for an adult has 13 headings; we will go one by one. The first point is the preparation that has to precede the examination. The preparation has to be taken by the patient, and there are things that have to be observed by the patient in terms of diet and behavior. The reason why one has to observe a certain diet and a certain behavior is because certain kinds of food, like light or cool food, and certain kinds of behavior, like exertion, all of these affect the natural pulse. They can change the pulse because of their action. The day before the examination is going to take place the patient should abstain from meat, beer, and hard liquor. The reason is that these three things create heat in the body. Food that has gone bad should be avoided, and one should not eat raw food. The kinds of meat we are referring to here is the meat that creates heat in the body, and other foods that create heat in the body. One meat which is considered to create cold in the body is goat's meat. If one eats meat that creates heat in the body, then the body will reflect that and the pulse will change. This also goes for cold-creating meat; then also the pulse will change. Goat, chicken, and buttermilk, as well as drinking too much water or juice, has an effect on the body in that it creates cold and changes the pulse.

This goes for the diet in terms of food and drink. Now as for behavior, the person should not exert the body too much the day before one is going to have an examination. Also, one should not sleep in the sun. One should not overeat or have an empty stomach for a long time, which means one should not have undereaten. The person should abstain from worrying, intense talk, and sexual intercourse. And, one should sleep well before coming for examination. These are the four main aspects of behavior. This completes the first point.

The second point is the time when the examination of the pulse should take place. One should examine the pulse when the sun is already in the sky, but the earth has not yet received the heat of the sun, there is no warmth coming yet. If it is a very windy day, then for a person with the prominent element of air, the breathing will be different and this will create disturbance in the person's natural pulse. That is not a convenient time to measure the pulse. Avoid examination of the pulse in full sun or in the middle of the night when the moon has come out, because this is too cold and the element of cold is predominant. When it is too hot or too cold, examination should be avoided.

Why is this to be observed? If the weather is cold, then the outer coldness will reflect in the body as a pulse which might be mistaken for a diseases of *bad-kan* and cold. The doctor might make the wrong diagnosis. Because the patient is cold, the blood decreases and the doctor might think that the patient has a problem of deficient blood. If one examines the patient when the weather is too hot, because of the outer heat the pulse might indicate a fever. Or, because the blood goes up when there is heat, the doctor might think that there is a problem of too much blood or high blood pressure.

This behavior and diet applies to everybody, whether one is very sick or not very sick but having some kind of problem. This consideration of the time of day is most important for those people with a very serious disease, for others it is not so important. In connection to this, the patient should observe that when he or she is coming to be examined they should not be puffing because of exertion. In that case, the breath has become exaggerated as the patient has been exerting himself or herself. Then the patient should rest until the breath is more normal and then the patient can be examined.

It is important to have the right position of the arm during the examination. It is not right for the doctor to be standing and holding the arm without caring about the position of the patient's arm. The patient should not be lying down. The patient should be sitting up and the arm of the patient extended with the back of the palm down.

The third point has to do with the position where the pulse is examined in the stages of examination. If one starts to count from the first wrinkle on the wrist of the patient, the doctor should tightly place the fingers a distance from the wrinkle which is equivalent to the length of half of the patient's thumb.

The three fingers of each of the doctor's hands will determine the pulse. The three fingers are index, middle and ring finger. When these three fingers are placed on the arm of the patient, they should not be touching each other and they should not be separated too much. The tips of the fingers should be in line.

There is a life vein which indicates the life of the patient, which is a dark vein in the middle of the arm. When that is measured, one can determine whether the patient is going to die or not. If one is not able to detect that pulse of life, the doctor cannot identify that pulse in the arm. Before concluding that the patient will die, the doctor should consult another point which is in a bone in the ball of the foot. This life-vein is localized there. When it cannot be detected there, then it is sure that the patient will die. When it can be detected in the foot, but not in the arm, then there is a way of treatment for the patient; it is not an absolute indication that the patient will die.

The fourth point is connected to the amount of pressure that these six fingers should exert on the arm of the patient. The index should press down to the level of the skin. The middle finger should press down to the flesh. The ring finger should press all the way down to the bone. The reason for this is because the shape of the arm is like a radish. That means that it is fatter downwards and goes thinner towards the wrist; therefore, when we are applying pressure we have to press harder where the fatter part of the arm is.

The doctor has to have several qualifications or characteristics of his or her hands in order to do a correct reading. The doctor should have soft hands, clean and free of warts. They should also be warm hands.

Also, the doctor should be free of three diseases: asthma, trembling, and of *rlung*. If the doctor is sick with any of these three kinds of illnesses, then the reading will be disturbed. When the doctor has a problem with *rlung*, it usually manifests as nervousness; because of that, the doctor cannot determine accurately the messages from the pulse. It would be a bit like talking with a crazy person on the telephone. One does not really understand or make out what they are trying to say. The doctor needs concentration when he or she checks the patient. The doctor should be able to concentrate strongly on the pulse. So if he or she is nervous or has a problem with *rlung*, then the doctor would have many thoughts and it would be difficult to conduct an examination.

The second case is when the doctor is trembling. The pulse is a very subtle, fine kind of indication, so if the hand of the doctor is already trembling before he or she starts to read the pulse, then the doctor will create a disturbance in the pulse and read the wrong thing.

The fifth point is the method for examining each of the pulses. When the patient extends the left arm to be examined by the doctor, this is a good omen. The doctor starts by examining that extended arm.

In different texts, there is also another type of indication which is done in relation to how one should start measuring the pulse. In this text, it says that if the patient is a man, one should start with the left arm, and if the patient is a woman, to start with the right arm. The text states that the reason for this is that in a man, his right side is like method and his left side is more like wisdom. This is reversed in the case of a woman. So, by doing an examination this way, one is making method and wisdom united. There is really no difference between these systems, and one should just accept them.

We will start now, as we said before, with the patient putting his or her left arm out. The doctor will examine the pulse of the patient with the three fingers of the right hand. Each of the three fingers that the doctor is using has two different types of feeling. These are located up and down in an imaginary line that runs in the middle of the finger.

We will start with the index finger. The upper part of the index finger reads the heart and the lower part of the index finger reads the intestines. As we said before when we examined the body, there are five main organs and six hollow organs which the six fingers can read in the pulse.

With the upper part of the middle finger of the right hand, one can measure the condition of the spleen. With the lower part of this finger, the doctor can determine whether there is sickness in the stomach.

The upper part of the ring finger can read the condition of the left kidney. The lower part reads the state of the uterus in the case of a woman, and the seminal vessels in the case of a man.

So, after reading the pulse with the right hand on the left arm of the patient, the doctor should change arms and read, with the left hand, the right arm of the patient. The three fingers that we use are the same: ring, middle and index.

The index of the left hand of the doctor is also divided into two. The upper part reads the functioning of the lungs while the lower part reads the state of the large intestines.

With the middle finger, the upper part indicates the state of the liver and the lower part indicates the gall bladder.

The upper part of the ring finger reads the right kidney, and with the lower part it reads the urinary bladder, which is the same whether the patient is a man or a woman.

If the patient is a woman, the index finger will read the opposite of what we said before. The heart of a woman is a little bit more toward the right, and the heart of a man is more toward the left.

We will start now with the sixth heading. This point has to do with what we talked about before as the constant or natural pulse of the individual. When the being is born, it has three basic emotions: passion, aggression, and desire. As a result of these emotions, then a person has a characteristic pulse which does not change, it is the natural pulse.

There are three different categories of this pulse, which divides into either male, female, or neutral pulse. The male pulse arises mainly from the factor of *rlung*, or *prana*, and it is similar to that pulse of *rlung*. The way of pulsating is swollen and it is also coarse. The female pulse has the nature of *mkhris-pa* or bile, and its way of beating is fast and subtle. Finally, the neutral pulse has the nature of *bad-kan*, or phlegm, and its characteristic beat is that it is slow and soft. We will talk a bit about how these interact in a couple. If both members of the couple have a male pulse, then most of the offspring will be boys. If both have a female pulse, then most of the children will be girls. If one has female pulse and the other a male pulse, then they will have children of both sexes. If both have a neutral pulse, generally speaking neutral pulse procreate less, so if both have a neutral pulse then they will have maybe one boy but then no more children. There is no rule that men should have a male pulse or women should have a female pulse. This male and female pulse comes equally to both men and women. If a man has a female pulse, this indicates he will have a long life. If a man has a male pulse, this indicates that his partner can have many children. Whoever has the neutral pulse will have a long life and also a healthy body without disease; those who have a higher status than him or her will praise them, but those who are lower will be jealous. Uncles and aunts of the person's family will not like this person with neutral pulse. If both people have a neutral pulse, then they will have just one boy. He will not be able to procreate and thus the whole blood lineage will come to an end.

Now we will look into the seventh headline, and this is examination of the pulse in accordance with the seasons. It is important and it is essential to have this kind of consideration of the seasons of the year, because just as the outer weather changes this also reflects in the body of the individual, according to that outer condition. It is like when trees, plants, fruits, and so forth change according to the seasons, it also brings changes in the body of the individual. If it is very hot, then this reflects in the pulse as a certain characteristic. If it is very cold, this effects the pulse in a way that is strictly due to the outside weather, not by the individual.

Let us now start with the springtime. In each of the seasons, we will consider the season's length to be 72 days. Actually, we say three months for each season. We will consider, when we are saying springtime, or summer, or autumn, or winter, that we are talking about the first 72 days of these three months, leaving 18 days in each cycle. These we will explain later.

So, springtime. Springtime is the time when grass starts to grow in the fields, and trees start to develop leaves and flowers. In springtime, when the outer condition is spring, then the inner reaction is of the element of wood, which is mostly related with liver. Then the liver becomes stronger just because it is spring. The characteristic of that pulse is that it would be subtle, but the beat would be long, with long intervals.

The remaining 18 days of springtime or of any other season is related with the element of earth and this reflects in the functioning of the spleen. The pulse of the spleen at this time becomes short and piercing.

Now for the season of summer. Summertime is when the flowers bloom and the weather is rainy. This season is connected with the element of fire; because of the nature of the element of fire, the internal organ is affected is the heart. And so the pulse of the heart changes. The characteristic of the pulse at this time will be swollen and easy to feel and detect.

The remaining 18 days would be just as we said before for springtime. They would be related to the spleen and react as we said before.

The next season is autumn. Autumn is defined as the time of the year when fruit comes to maturation, ripens. This reflects inside the body in the organ which is connected to the element of iron, which is the lungs. So the pulse of the lungs becomes stronger during this season. The characteristic of this pulse is that it will be short and rough. Just as we said before, the remaining 18 days are the pulse of spleen.

The season of winter is defined as that time of year when earth and water freeze. That was the characteristic of Tibet, in other parts of the world maybe this does not happen in this way, but this is the cold season. At that time, the internal organ which is influenced by the weather change is the kidneys. The characteristic of the pulse at this time of year would be that each beat would be short and soft. Then, as we said before, the remaining 18 days of the season are the days of the spleen, connected to the element of earth.

Now we start with the eighth headline. We will now make a division between whether the person is a healthy person or whether the person has a disease. We start by the examination of the pulse of a person who is healthy. While examining the person, it is important to consider the influence of the outer condition of the season of the year. This is because if, for example, it is one of the remaining 18 days of a season, then the spleen would cause a more short and piercing pulse then the beats of the other organs. If the doctor forgets that he or she is reading the pulse at that point in that season, then the doctor may diagnose a problem with the spleen, the heart or the liver. What is actually happening is that they are reaching to the outer circumstances; if the doctor then prescribes medicine because he or she thinks the patient is sick, then the doctor is making a big mistake.

The person is classified as a healthy person when the doctor is examining the person's constant pulse, taking a measurement of time which is the time it takes the doctor to inhale, to keep the breath, and then exhale. If the constant pulse beats five times during the whole cycle of the doctor's breath, then the person can be said to be healthy. When we are considering a child, the child's pulse is usually faster than an adult, so it should beat seven times in order for the child to be considered healthy. If it is difficult to measure the breath, then we can measure the time as one minute. If there are around 75 beats in a minute then the person is considered to be healthy. A healthy child's heart would beat 110 or so per minute. This is not an all-sufficient condition for the person to be considered healthy. Still we have to examine the pulse and the pulse should be free of six defects. The pulse should not be too strong or too soft. The pulse also should not be too sunken or too protruding. It should not be hard or tight, and also it should not be a pulse that cannot be detected, is unnoticeable. If the pulse is free of these six defects and at the same time the person's heartbeat is five times in a whole breath, then the person can be considered healthy, even though he might have a cold or some minor affliction. That does not mean that the person is unhealthy or needs to take special medicine. The functioning of the whole body in this case is proper.

If in the whole breath cycle of the doctor, the beat of the patient is seven, eight, or nine, then this indicates a problem of the heat or of fever. If the beat is four, three, or two, then that beat indicates a problem of cold.

In this way, there are three types or degrees of fever: strong, medium, then light fever. The same with cold; there are strong, medium and light degrees. The strong fever is when there are nine beats to the breath cycle. If this is the case then there is danger that the person may have a hemorrhage in the brain or that some of his or her limb actions could become paralyzed. A beating of eight indicates a medium fever. There is no danger, but still medication has to be taken. Light fever, which is the beat of seven, is quite common. It can come because of a simple flu, or because one has eaten the wrong kind of food, or done the wrong kind of thing.

If the pulse beats twice in one breath cycle of the doctor, then this indicates the worst kind of cold. Three beats is a medium cold and is not so bad; it can be cured with medicine, with treatment. When the pulse beats four times, then this indicates that the person is not suffering from anything very serious. The person may have been standing in a cold wind, otherwise he or she ate too many raw, cold-producing foods and has a problem of digestion in the stomach, but it is not so bad.

The next headline is examination of the pulse of a sick person. Under this headline, one examines the 424 kinds of diseases which arises as result of an imbalance of *rlung*, *mkhris-pa* and *bad-kan*. One can divide these 424 main diseases into two main kinds. These two are problems of cold and problems of heat. In each there are six kinds of beats in the pulse. Six beats for fever, six beats for cold.

For the strongest kind of fever, the pulse indicates this as a very full pulse with a strong beat. The second kind of fever, medium fever, is shown in the beat of a pulse which is rolling, full and also fast. The lowest kind of fever has a pulse which is twisting and hard. We have seen that there are two kinds of qualities in each of these pulses. This completes the examination of the fever or heat pulse.

The worst of the cold diseases shows in the pulse as being very sunken and weak. Sunken means that one has to press very hard to detect it, and weak means that is very soft and it does not have much strength. The second, medium kind of cold has a pulse that is flat and slow. With the last kind of cold, the lowest kind, the pulse is loose and hollow. When the pulse beats in the upper part, that indicates an old or chronic case of cold. When it is beating in the lower part, that means that it is new, that the disease is fresh.

Now we are going to examine pulses which are specific disorders, which indicate specific kinds of disease, but for this the doctor should keep clearly in mind all the pulses which we have talked about. Otherwise, the pulses may beat very much alike and if the doctor does not make a note of it with the first approach, which is more general, then he or she may become confused. What the doctor has to keep in mind now is the characteristics of the six kinds of fever and the six kinds of cold, that makes 12, and then there are four pulses of disease, that makes 16. And then there is the three pulses of the constant pulse: female, male and neutral. The doctor must keep these in mind in the beginning.

Now, in this next headline the characteristic beats of the different disease are examined. We start with the pulse of *rlung* which has the characteristic of being hollow or empty. That means that one feels the pulse, presses down, then one realizes that it is hollow; the person has a disease of only *rlung*. The second is when the person has a bile disease, then the pulse is very subtle and the doctor will feel that is tight and twisted. This does not mean that there is something twisted in there, but just that this is how it feels. The characteristic of the pulse of the person who has only the disease of *bad-kan* or phlegm is that the pulse will be sunken, found only after pressing, and that it will be flat and without strength.

There is another category of disease which comes about when these three are coupled with each other. This is called *ldan-pa*. When fever is combined with *rlung*, then the pulse that results is one that beats fast, but is hollow. Another combination is *bad-kan* and bile. The characteristic of the *bad-kan* pulse is sunken, and of bile pulse is subtle and fast. When these two are together, *bad-kan* and bile, then the pulse that results is sunken and also subtle, meaning fast.

When we consider another type of disease is *de-mug-po* of the stomach. It produces a kind of beat which is swollen and full. If this *mug-po* is located in the liver, then it is cancer of the liver. If it is localized in the lungs, then it is called tuberculosis. *Mug-po* in general is a disease of phlegm.

We have just mentioned a few example of the category of the diseases of *ldan-pa* when two are acting at the same time. Now we will continue mentioning some other diseases. For instance, there are many problems of the blood, whether it is high blood pressure or low blood pressure, or whether the blood is impure, bad blood and so forth. Each of these can be determined by the examination of the pulse, but we cannot really go into the examination of them because of lack of time. In general the pulse of a problem of blood is rolling, like touching the bead of a rosary. It is kind of protruding, that kind of feeling. Protruding and rolling, those two are the characteristics of the blood problems.

If the woman is pregnant then this reflects in the pulse of the kidney rolling as protruding, as we said before. Of course, the pulse of the kidney is measured with a different finger than that of examining the blood.

When there is a problem of serum, or waste fluid, which is localized in any part of the body, according to which part there are certain characteristics in the pulse. Generally speaking, say in the case of a boil or blister or sore inside the body, then this problem of serum or water manifests in the pulse as trembling and also one can feel that circulation is impeded.

Another pulse that is interesting to talk about is the pulse of a problem of worms, including germs, bacteria, or whatever. Inside the body there are all kinds of beings like worms or bacteria, and the general term would be worms or germs. We can reduce them to three kinds of worms. One of them is like round worm, it is long and round. Another one is like tape worm. Then the third kind is like hook worm, which is very small and the head is very strong. These three kinds of worms subsume the same kind of ability of all the different germs that exist in the body. The general pulse which indicates worms would be flat and also it will beat as when we see a snake moving up. There is also a feeling that the doctor experiences the pulses is kind of pulled up, pinching.

With the pulse of leprosy, when one touches the pulse then half of the pulse does not seem to exist; one feels this part, and then the other half seems to exist. It is like half of the vein is beating and half is not. It has a feeling like the pulse itself is trembling, shaking.

These are the pulses of the common diseases. When there is a wound in the body, this reflects in the pulse, and it becomes swollen and hard. Then the pulse is also very fast. With this kind of pulse, one can determine if the person has been stabbed or if a person has been attacked with a certain weapon. Or, also, if the person has been shot, one can determine where the bullet is inside the body.

Perhaps I have not been very clear, but I am talking about two different pulses. One is to determine if there is a wound in the body. Now, this is to determine if there is pain in the body as a result of the wound. One can determine where the bullet is by examining with the six fingers the pulses of the different organs of the body, and also the right and left side of the body. In this way we can pinpoint it. The feeling of this pulse is like two beats in union.

After an accident one can have injury just to the skin, the flesh, or it can go to the head, the cranium, or even damage the brain. With the three fingers, one can determine the degree of the injury that has happened to the head. If the injury is internal, but it has only affected the flesh and the skin, then the pulse is registered with the index fingers and the pulse would be very strong. When there is damage in the bone, in the cranium, then the middle finger registers the pulse as kind of twisting. When there is brain damage, then this is registered in the ring finger as a pulse that is very fast.

When there is infection, there can be accumulation of pus in any part of the body; it can be in the arm, in the hands, it can also be in an internal organ. When one is measuring with six fingers, a different organ for each finger, then one can determine where the infection is by remembering the normal pulse of that organ. In case of infection, then there will be the extra element of trembling and of heat.

The eleventh heading is how with the three fingers we divide the body, which fingers can register the functioning of the different parts of the body.

The two index fingers register the functioning of the heart, the chest, the sense organs in the head; all the five sense organs up to the crown of the head. The middle fingers register the functioning of the part of the body between the lower part of the heart and the upper part of the kidneys, including the stomach, the skin of the stomach and all the organs there. With the ring fingers one measures all the parts of the body which lie from the kidneys, including the kidneys, all the way down to the tip of the toes. This means the back, the coxae, the legs, and also the toes.

The twelfth headline deals with the four relationships, which are called mother, son, friend, and foe. We will do this very briefly. Since I am a mother, let us start with the mother relationship. Let us consider the influence of the outer elements as it is reflected in the inner elements of the body. I am now talking about the qualities of the elements within one's own body, that characteristic or that energy within one's own body. We start with wood and the mother of wood is water. The mother of water is iron. The mother of iron is earth. The mother of earth is fire. The mother of fire is wood, and thus we complete the cycle. Now let us talk about the relationship of son. The son of wood is fire. The son of fire is earth. The son of earth is iron.

The son of iron is water, and the son of water is wood. Seeing them in one direction is seeing the mother. In the other direction it is the son.

If one writes these in the form of a cross, then horizontally one can draw the relationship between mother and son. Vertically, one can draw the relationship of friend with foe.

Let us now see what this friend and foe is. The foe of wood is iron. The foe of iron is fire. The foe of fire is water. The foe of water is earth. The foe of earth is wood. Then, the friend of wood is earth. The friend of earth is water. The friend of water is fire. The friend of fire is iron. And the friend of iron is wood.

Then, at this point we should also consider the seven astonishing pulses. This actually is a very long subject, but I will only give an example for explanation. For these seven astonishing pulses, one should examine a person who is healthy, who does not have any diseases. There is all kinds of information that can come from examining this pulse. These astonishing pulses can indicate what can happen to other persons related to the person who is being examined: the mother, father, friend, foe and so forth. There are many combinations of these and I will cite an example. Let us consider the case of a woman who comes to be examined and we want to determine the condition of her mother.

Say the mother is sick and is taken to the hospital, so the daughter comes to the doctor to be examined for her mother. The first condition is that the daughter should be without any sickness. Since the mother is the element of water in the body of the daughter, and that organ is the kidney. One examines then the pulse of the kidneys of the daughter. If the pulse of the daughter's kidney is slow and flat, then this indicates that the mother's liver is weak. If it is pulsating full and strong, then this indicates that there is fever in the mother and also a problem of *rlung*, of *prana*. If it is tight and unnoticeable, then this indicates that the mother is under the influence of the strength of evil spirits. When this pulse, still of the daughter's kidney pulse, is pulsating and the touch is hot to the doctor's, then this indicates that the mother has an infection in one of the internal organs.

If the daughter is sick, then one examines the mother. The son of wood is fire. We say that the relationship of the daughter to the mother is that the daughter is the heart of the mother. When one is examining the mother to determine the condition of the daughter, then the pulse of the mother's heart is examined. This is because the element of the heart is fire and the son of wood is fire. If the daughter has fever, then the mother's pulse will be strong, fierce, and full. A problem of cold in the daughter will reflect in the mother's heart pulse as being very slow, sunken, and without strength. If the daughter has a problem of *rlung*, then the heart beat on the mother's arm is hollow. We have seen now the relationship for mother and daughter; for father and son, it is the same.

There are other types, seven total types of astonishing pulse, and one could elaborate on them for a whole day, so we move instead to the thirteenth headline.

Now we will talk about the pulse of death. This will be interesting, for it involves all the different elements of the person who is going to die and their relationship to the pulse. When this pulse of the person beats like the flapping of a flag—when in all the pulses of the person this quality is found, then this indicates that the person is going to die from a problem of *rlung*. When the person is going to die from a problem of bile, then the pulse is as follows. There is a bird, I don't know how to translate it, *trah*, it is sort of a falcon, a big bird that eats small prey. When it has located its prey it flaps its wings back and forth very quickly, and this is the example of how the heat of the pulse is of the person who is going to die of bile. Another characteristic is that the pulse is trembling and is full of pulsation. The pulse of a person who is going to die of *bad-kan* is similar to the saliva of a sow. The cow is eating and a lot of saliva is produced and falls down to the earth. The beat is like that.

This can be seen in the pulse, but we can also see signs of this in the body of the person who is about to die. The heart and the tongue are connected, so when the heart starts to lose its power, that means getting closer to death. This manifests as a shortening or a contraction of the tongue. The person who is dying cannot talk very properly because the tongue has become contracted. If the person is dying from some disease, then this has already shortened the tongue, but the characteristic now is that it even becomes shorter. When the liver starts to fail, then since the liver and the eyes are connected, this is shown in the eyes that the person does not move the eyes anymore. They are mostly looking up and there is no movement. The spleen is connected with the lips, so when this is failing, this is shown in that the person cannot keep his or her mouth closed and the lower lip just falls down. Even when the person closes the mouth for a moment, then the lower lip again falls down. When the lungs fail, since they are connected to the nose, the nostrils close, become contracted. The kidneys are connected with the ears, so when the pulse of the kidneys cease, then the ears are no longer able to hear. You may be talking to the person, then suddenly they can no longer hear you.

Even when a person is healthy and does not have a problem, he or she could still, by checking the ears, determine if there was a great obstacle awaiting that could terminate their life suddenly. First one inserts the two index fingers and blocks the ears. In a silent place, we should block both ears with the index fingers, and if we hear a humming then that means that there is no problem or danger for our life. If we hear no humming at all, this indicates that we might die soon.

Of course the doctor checks the pulse in our arm, but we can also examine the shadow that our hand and our body cast. We examine the shadow that is cast by the moon in the night. This is the best time, but otherwise the second best is under the sun. First one looks at the shadow of the whole body as it is cast by the moon. If that shadow does not have a head, then this indicates that one might die. This first exercise is done while standing.

For the second one, we sit down and put our arm this way. if we look at the shadow and there is no image of the arm, there is an empty space where the arm should be, it means that we will die very quickly.

When we take a bath and our skin is still wet, we can also check with the wetness on the body. After coming out of the bath and the body is still wet, if the region of the heart becomes dry very quickly, as if it has never been wet, then that indicates that the person will die.

This is only a small example of what is said about the signs of death. There are many, many other examples, but maybe if we talk too much you will become doubtful.

Now we have briefly completed the subject.

17

Urine Diagnosis

The second examination in Tibetan medicine is done by observing the urine. One examines the urine in nine different ways, nine points. If the patient does not observe certain conditions in the diet, then it might cause a change in the color of the urine. So, the patient should observe the correct diet before examination. One should avoid foods that have the nature of cold, like cold foods, and also coffee or tea, beer or hard liquor, and sour things. The first thing about avoiding cold food is because it effects the *rlung* and the phlegm.

The second consideration is that the person should go to bed about midnight. The next morning the person should get up and, without having eaten anything, he or she should urinate. The person should not waste that urine; he or she should collect that urine to bring it to the doctor.

The second point is the time that one should examine the urine. It should not be done in the night, it should be done in the daytime when the sun is up already because to examine the color, the steam, and so forth, one needs sunlight.

The third point is the container where one is going to examine the urine. It should be without any color, either transparent or white. If one uses something to stir the urine, it should be white. It could be like a stick or a chopstick, but it must be white.

Now the method for examination of the urine. The examination is done while the urine is still hot, when the patient has just urinated. The best way of examining the urine is when it is hot, because the smell is the strongest and also the steam is more pronounced at this time. So at that time, it is best to analyze the steam and the smell. When it has become lukewarm, that is the best time to examine the sediment. The best time to check the way the urine has settled and the colors change is when the urine has become cold. These certain characteristics of the color when the urine is cold do not appear when the urine is hot or lukewarm. There is a sediment that forms in the urine, and if there is a lot of sediment which is very thick it means that there is a problem of fever or heat. If there is only a little sediment, that indicates that there is a problem of cold. If there is a lot of steam, that indicates fever. Otherwise, if there is little steam, this indicates cold. If the smell is strong, that indicates fever. If the smell is not strong, this indicates cold.

The fourth point is the examination of the urine of a person who has no sickness. At the time that the urine is hot, it is light yellow. We compare this color in our tradition with the color of melted butter made from the milk of the *dri*, which is a cross between a yak and a cow. This color of the *dri* butter is exactly the color of healthy urine. The the amount of steam from healthy urine is neither too much nor too little. The same holds for the smell. Also, the foam is formed of bubbles of an even size, neither too high nor too small.

Now with the fifth point, we deal only with the urine of a person who is sick. First, one observes the color. If the urine is a bluish kind of liquid, that means that there is a problem of rLung. If the urine is orange color, a strong yellow, this indicates a problem of bile. If the urine is turbid, then it is a problem of *bad-kan*.

What is turbid? When you put a piece of cheese in water the water becomes sort of whitish. Similarly when in the liver the blood has become too pronounced or there is a problem of blood, then there is a reddish color in the urine. This color is translated literally as the color you get when you use a red dye. Urine of a reddish color indicates a problem of blood. When the color is pinkish, then there is a problem of the waste water in the body, like serum. If the urine has an ochre color, a dark yellow, this means that the person has a problem in the stomach. He or she cannot digest food properly. If this is not treated, then the stomach can become hard and this hardening can develop into a tumor, and from a tumor into cancer.

We have considered now examples of kind of individual cases. Now we will see when there is a combination of diseases together. If the urine is whitish and yellowish, then it is a problem of phlegm and bile combined. If the urine has a color that is bluish and yellowish, then it is a combination of a problem of *rlung* and of bile. When there is a bluish and a reddish tinge in the urine, this is a problem of *rlung* and blood. A reddish and yellowish tinge is a problem of bile and of blood. When it is whitish like water with cheese in it, then that indicates phlegm and cold. When there is a whisk of white in the urine, that means that there is a discharge of the body into the urine. When it is reddish with a tinge of yellow, this indicates a problem or a tightness in the back. When the urine is tinged black as if we had dropped some ink into water, this means that the person has poison in the system, it has already ripened and the person will die. However, the problem of poison in the system can also show up in the urine in many different colors like a rainbow. At that point, although it is poisoning, it can be treated and it can be cured.

The sixth point now is to examine the steam of the urine. When there is a lot of steam and it stays for a long time, then this indicates that there is a chronic case of fever that is fresh. There is steam, but it does not stay too long or too little. When the steam does not stay but disappears almost at once, then this indicates a very bad case of cold which is firmly rooted. Then when there is steam that stays only for a little while. This also indicates a problem of cold. When there is steam but it comes at some point rising and at another point it is low, then this indicates a mixed problem of cold. When there is steam but it comes at one point rising and at another point it is low, then this indicates a mixed problem of cold and fever. It may be difficult to imagine that these two can coexist, but it does happen and it happens in many cases. For instance, the lower part of the body has problem of cold which could be rheumatism while the upper part of the body could be suffering from fever, which can manifest as high blood pressure. These can coexist in a person easily.

If the smell is strong, this indicates heat. If it is light, this indicates cold. When the urine smells like food, for instance if the person has eaten fruit or meat and the urine smells like fruit or meat, this indicates that the person's stomach is not digesting food properly. A problem of *rlung* shows in the urine as a musty kind of smell, like an old car that has rusted and smells musty. When the smell is like the smell of burnt barley flour, this indicates a problem of bile; it has a very pungent smell, like ammonia. The smell that the urine has when there is a problem of *bad-kan*, is the same smell that one finds in the lice taken off a dog. A dog who has lice has a special smell; this is that smell. The smell of the urine of one who has a problem of the three humors combined together, is like cooked, burnt fat in direct contact with fire. If there is a smell of blood in the urine, that means that there is a problem of blood. If it smells like pus, that means that one of the internal organs is infected. Some other time, we don't have time now, we will bring all these different things and burn these things, bring in a dog with lice, everything to explain the smells.

The seventh point is examination of the bubbles, of the froth.

When the bubbles are big and globular like the eyes of a cow, then it is a problem of *rlung*. If the bubbles are very small, then it is a problem of bile. When the bubbles make noise, that is a problem of *rlung* and heat. This is talking about right after the person has urinated, the bubbles make a certain noise. There is an inflammation in the body, and it results in these bubbles' noise. If the bubbles in the urine are like when we blow spittle, then the problem is one of *bad-kan*, of phlegm. If it is like sand in the urine, there is a problem with the kidneys.

Now the eighth point. When we look at the color of the urine we might jump to certain conclusions just because of the color. In order to avoid confusion or mistake, this eighth point is prescribed. When there is a problem of liver, kidneys, or spleen, in general terms the urine has a reddish tinge. For problems with the large intestines, the urinary bladder, or the main hollow organs, the urine is whitish.

Now we will talk about the last point, the ninth point, the urine that indicates death. If the person has internal bleeding and is going to die from this, then the urine reflects this by separating in different sections. It forms in different parts like the blood is separating. If the person is going to die from a problem of phlegm, then this shows in the urine as like when milk separates or goes bad. If the person is going to die from a problem of bile, then the color of the urine will be yellowish, but it will also be separating into different parts. There is a certain disease which is very bad in terms of the urine, this is when the person urinates only intermittently and the smell is very bad and foul. This indicates a terminal disease.

We said at first that there are three main types of examination for diagnosis. The first was by contact with the pulse. The second by examining the urine. The third one is questioning the patient.

18

Medicine, Treatment, Diet and Behavior

We have seen the three types of techniques which are utilized in Tibetan medicine for diagnosis. Today we deal with the subjects of medicine, treatment, diet and behavior. Let us then start with the subject of medicine. In the subject of medicine, we will mention the different kinds of medicines that are used and also the potency of each kind.

The first kind that we will examine is that made of precious substances. There are two kinds of precious substances that we will consider. One kind of precious substances or jewels are those that can be melted. The other kind cannot be melted. In the first category are gold, silver, and so forth. In the second category, those that cannot be melted would be coral, turquoise, pearl and so forth.

The second kind of medicine are those made from earth, then there is from stone, wood, roots, leaves, flowers, fruits, bark, sap and from certain animals.

All these different categories of medicine differ from each other in terms of taste and also of potency, ability, and power. There are about a thousand kinds of medicines; if we were to go deeply into each of these there would not be enough time. So, we will just briefly mention medicines that have the five elements, or the qualities of the five elements. Most medicines have the basic element of earth and water and the taste that results is a sweet taste. Most medicines that are formed from fire and earth primarily have the taste of sourness. From the elements of water and fire, these medicines have predominantly a salty taste. Air and water result in a bitter taste. Air and fire together, when predominant in a medicine, result in a hot taste. Earth and air give the result of an astringent taste. In this way, we have seen the six kinds of taste and their relationship to six tastes.

Now let us see the qualities that each of the medicines have in connection with the tastes. Medicines that are mostly of the element of earth have a characteristic or quality that is heavy, stale, smooth and also kind of dull. It is also dry and oily. Medicine that has a predominance of the element of water is liquid and cool, oily, heavy and flexible. Because of this quality, for instance if one has liquid in the body, the reaction is liquefying, oily, heavy. Not only the quality of the medicine, but also the effect that it has on the body. It is better to translate is that way. For instance, when we say that medicines of earth are stable or firm, that means that they produce stability in the body. Medicines that come from earth are good for treating diseases that come from *bad-kan*.

Medicines that come from water are moistening, they create more moisture in the body. They kind of unify everything because of this liquefying ability. The medicines that originate from water are good for the treatment of diseases of bile and of the heart.

Medicines that originate primarily from fire elements are heat-producing and also sharpening, drying, and roughing, lightening, and they give mobility. Just as medicines from earth produce firmness and medicines from water produce wetness, then the function of the medicines of fire is to bring about warmth of the body. With heat to the stomach, digestion is aided and warmth also gives color to the skin. Primarily, these medicines from fire are used to treat disturbances of *bad-kan*.

With medicines where air is predominant, they are lightening; they give mobility, they are roughening, cooling, absorbing and drying. The effect of these medicines that have predominant *rlung* is that they give firmness and energy to the body, and the sense organs are sharpened. T they give strength to the mind, in the sense of courage and determination. These kinds of medicines are used to clear treatment of *rlung* and of bile. The disease of *rlung*, generally speaking, can change into any of the diseases of bile and Phlegm. It is not so much changing but invading other types of diseases. For instance, if there is a disease of phlegm, *rlung* invades to make a compound disease of *bad-kan* and *rlung*. It can also combine easily with bile and make a compound disease of *rlung* and bile.

Other medicines originate predominantly from the element of space. When we see a plant, the plant is usually hollow. When we see vegetables that are mostly hollow, these plants arise mainly from the element of space. These types of medicines can treat combined diseases of three humors together. They have an effect on the mind of the patient. If the patient's mind is worried and so forth, then it makes the mind very open and clear. And it also makes the mind very happy.

There are many categories of medicines, and each category also has many, many different types of medicines, so it would take too much time to mention all of them. It would be like saying 'Holland' but in 'Holland' there are many cities and towns. So, we will mention just the most important categories and leave aside the less important.

In each category of medicine that we will deal with, I will only mention the best. There are 13 kinds of medicines that treat problems of *rlung*. The ingredients are materials like nutmeg. For diseases of the combination of a problem of *rlung* and heat, one utilizes eight different medicines. One ingredient is a creeper plant like ivy. *rLung* is combined with heat and this has the effect like the creeper that can grow very fast and cover a large area. It creates this kind of effect on the problem of *rlung* and heat. For a problem of heat, fever, one utilizes white sandalwood and many other things. There are 11 different kinds of ingredients used. There are 20 kinds of medicine used for the treatment of *bad-kan*, among these is pomegranate.

There are 14 kinds of medicine used for the treatment of heat and *bad-kan* combined, among these is *chung-she*, which is like a stone. For the treatment of inflammations, then one uses 23 kinds of medicines, among these a yellow flower that does not grow in the west, *zer-me*. For the clearing of the diseases of bile, one ingredient is called *dzati* which is like ginseng. For problems of cold, one uses medicines from saffron and other things; there are 13 kinds of medicines. For the treatment of serum or waste fluids in the body, then one uses eight kinds of medicines.

We mention here only one of the ingredients used in the medicines. It is like if we just mention the name of one person here, still all these other people are here! All the other ingredients in the medicines are used.

For the treatment of diarrhea there are 17 kinds of medicines and one ingredient is kind of a liquid sweat that oozes out of rocks. For the treatment of drops, medicines are given to dry out; there are 17 kinds of ingredients, one of which is a flower that is sort of like a dwarf rhododendron. For poisoning, there are 16 kinds of medicines and one of them is a plant that looks like the paw of an eagle.

As for laxatives, there could be constipation because of a heat or cold in the body. Let us first consider constipation from a problem of heat. There are six kinds of medicines to create a gentle laxative. One of these is one of the five myrobalan I mentioned before. The begging bowl of the Buddha of Medicine is filled in the center with this myrobalan. As a fierce laxative, there are another six medicines, and one of the main ingredients is like a small black pea. To induce vomiting, there are nine kinds of medicines; among the ingredients is white mustard seed.

For the treatment of the five organs, there are six kinds of noble or good medicine. They are called this because they are empowered, they are medicines with a greater potency to cure all diseases. They have qualities from all the different ingredients, the different medicines. For problems in the heart, one uses the medicines made of nutmeg, saffron for the liver, large brown cardamon is used for the spleen, clove is for the life-channel or the life-vein, and bamboo shoot is used for the problems with the lungs. For the treatment of kidneys, small green cardamon is used. Black pepper is for treatment of the stomach and digestion.

Now we will talk briefly about the ways the medicines are prepared. When we talk about medicines made of precious substances we say that they are classified into two categories, those that can be melted and those that cannot. I will put an example of how to prepare medicine with those substances that can be melted. We start off, for instance, with mercury. We put it into a pot that has three characteristics, a special pot. We will start to treat that mercury with three ingredients. One ingredient is black pepper. Another is a kind of white earth. The third one is something very hot. They are ground up and put in an equal amount to the mercury. If we start with one kilo of mercury, we must add one kilo of these ingredients, and this has to be stirred. It must be worked upon for four days. These ingredients have the faculty of absorbing and taking away the poisons in the mercury. The mercury at the beginning is white, then at the end of the treatment it becomes dark blue because all of the poisons have been absorbed into the ingredients. After this, one has to put the mercury with water and it is cooked, boiled. Also at this point three more ingredients are added. After this treatment the water and the mercury separate. The third treatment is that we take the mercury and mix it with sesame oil or mustard oil, one part to two parts. Then we boil it together for a long time. All through this procedure it has to be stirred, if it is not continually stirred the mercury will stick to the pot. Then after this, we pour the oil away and are left with the mercury. This mercury will be treated again with yellow sulphur. We have to keep boiling and stirring until the sulphur has lost the color and the smell; this indicates that the remaining poison has been extracted from the mercury. For one kilo of mercury we need one kilo of sulphur. After the treatment, we take what is left of the mercury and clean it well. The sulphur has to be treated in this same way beforehand in order to lose its own poisons. So, the sulphur first is treated until it has lost its color and smell and then it is mixed with the mercury. The sulphur is made into a powder and then spread like a bed of sulphur, so that the mercury will roll but be contained over the sulphur. The mercury is hot when we pour it and then these two ingredients become mixed. Then after mixing, we have to still continue mixing properly with a certain stone that we use. Then after mixing them completely, the yellow of the sulphur does not remain, and the white of the mercury does not remain. What remains is dark blue. At that point the mixture is called *gngul-chu btso-thal*, mercury. *Tso* means cooked, and *thal* means ashes because there is also ashes in the product that is formed. This is what we do when we prepare only one of the ingredients, mercury. When we use gold, we also have to treat it in the same laborious way. To make these medicines takes great deal of work and care.

Now we will give an example of one precious substance which cannot be melted. For turquoise, coral, and lapis lazuli, the way of clearing the impurities is essentially the same. Before throwing these substances into the water, we prepare the water with certain medicine that comes from tree. Then we boil this water for a long time. After one hour we throw away the water. Then we put another kind of medicine which comes from a flower into the water, in certain amounts depending on which medicine we are making, and then we boil the whole thing. We have thrown in the stones, not crushing them but putting them in just as they are. After we boiled them the second time, then we rinse the stone three times with cold water. Then we have to dry what is left in a place of clean earth where no animals like dogs and so forth have been. For each of these medicines that has one kind of precious substance, we have to add 25 other ingredients coming from different categories of medicine. We mix these together. There are many medicines made from precious substances and their procedure, the way of making them, is similar. It is a very specialized and somewhat complicated procedure.

The second kind of medicine that is used is called *thang*, which means concoction. In this, one mixes different herbs that have been picked at the right time. One mixes three ingredients, four, five, six, seven; there are many different kinds of *thang*. The way to do it is very simple. It is just like boiling tea. This is very widespread in the West where everyone is drinking alot of herbal tea. The different herbal teas have each a different kind of potency. When drinking these herbal teas the effect is quite similar to drinking these medicines called *thang*.

The third category of medicine is powdered medicine. It is more complicated to prepare than the concoction we just mentioned. For instance, if we are making powdered medicine for the treatment of pain in the stomach, we use the skin of myrobalan.

The next category, the fourth, is making pills. This is even more complicated. Each of the medicines has to be treated according to what we want to treat with them. If we are using cardamom we have to use only the inside because the outside has no value, and then we have to peel each one. There is no machine that can do this, it has to be done by hand. After treating each of the ingredients like this, we will mix maybe three, 13, or 25 ingredients to make one pill. The first step is to mix all of these ingredients together, to make them into powder and to mix them together. If this is not done properly, then each of these ingredients will maintain its own potency without combining with the rest. So, first they have to be completely mixed and this takes a long time, for grinding and mixing. After that it has to be left at rest for a whole day. After this, the person who is preparing the medicines has to clean his or her hands, and then begin again with mixing and grinding that medicine.

After this we make the pills. The pills can be made with machines. To dry these pills, if the pills are divided into those that produce heat and those that give cold, the heat pills should not be dried in the heat but should always be dried in the shade. Conversely, the cold-producing pills should be dried in direct sunlight.

Then the pills are put into a very long bag made of cotton cloth. Two people hold the cloth from each side and move it up and forth so that the pills roll from one side to the other side. This is done for a whole day. This last procedure is what is responsible for making the Tibetan medicine pills so hard. This procedure takes out all the small particles of air that are still in the pills. If air remains in the pill then it is prone to allow bacteria to go in, and then pills go bad.

The next type of medicine is like a gruel or a soup. This soup is prepared with rich ingredients that have a lot of substantial nutrition. For instance, marrow, bone, milk and fat and so forth. These are boiled with added ingredients and then given later like a soup to the patient. With this soup, many different diseases can be treated.

The medicines that derive mainly from roots have very substantial vitamins. There are five kinds. They have the same quality for the body as what we know as vitamins. They give strength to the body. For instance, ginseng is quite a well-known root. There are three kinds of root which are similar to ginseng.

They vary according to their potency. So, there are five different categories of roots and in each of them, there are many divisions.

Now we have finished the subject of medicine.

19

Miscellaneous Treatment

We will now talk about miscellaneous treatments. The first treatment is to induce laxative or to induce vomiting. Another treatment is treatment of pouring liquid into the nose like nose drops. There is also massage, applying compresses, bloodletting, moxa and golden needle or acupuncture. Then, there is application by local touch, and mineral baths or thermal baths. For diagnosis, one can insert this thin kind of spoon and take a sample from inside the body. One can localize the area for treatment. It is not so much treatment itself. There are 72 different implements utilized for operation inside the body. For instance in the case of breast cancer, one of the veins connected to the breast can be infected. The infection is localized between the bone and the flesh, in the tissue, and the spoon is inserted there. It moves like a coil and the pus is extracted without damaging the vein. I think that it works like a hyperdermic needle, but it is not working exactly like that. We call this implement a spoon, but it is not like a teaspoon. There are all kinds of designs.

At the beginning, I will start with moxa and acupuncture because I think it will be interesting to you. Moxa is used for the treatment of diseases of cold and the treatment of the diseases of *rlung*. Golden needle is used for problems of heat and for problems of bile, as well as for problems of waste fluid or serum, like sinusitis. The benefits of both, whether the application of moxa or the needle, are the same and the point of application is the same. However, one has to know beforehand by the other forms of diagnosis whether the person has a problem of heat or of cold. Based on that, the doctor will decide to do either moxa or golden needle.

If we touch the back of our necks there is something protruding. That would be the first vertebrae. If one locates this one, then it is easier to go down the spine. In some treatments with golden needle, the top of the needle is heated. If there is no golden needle, then other types of needle are all right. Then, one heats up the point. The first vertebra is the house, the abode, of *rlung*. Remember that the point is the same whether one uses moxa or golden needle. One uses this point for cases of madness, for when the body trembles, and so forth. I started with this first vertebra of the back because it is the easiest to locate. There are many points on the head and so forth that are used, but the points are difficult to find without a doctor. This vertebra is easy to find plus it is kind of a central point for the body. The points that are located in the vertebra are also easy to find because one does not need to draw lines in order to find the point, as the doctor has to do in the case of many other points. Thereafter, without mistake, one can find these points on the vertebra very easily.

In each vertebra, there is a central part like a knuckle here on my hand. If the disease is mild, one can apply heat or needle only here at that point. However, if the disease is very strong then the treatment must be applied to three points in a line at the same time. The distance from the center would be measured from the thumb of the doctor.

I will explain now what I mean by mild disease or strong disease in each case. For a case where a person cannot sleep well or feels very unhappy, or the body trembles, then the treatment would only be applied to one point. Then, we apply the treatment to the vertebra treatment at three points at the same time, when for instance the person was slightly disturbed before but now he or she is completely mad. Another case is when one cannot hear because of some problem of *rlung*. A third case is when the heart is beating very strongly and the patient has palpitations, or when one becomes paralyzed in the upper part of the body because of malfunction of *rlung*. Some people who are crazy cannot talk or produce crazy sounds. It is also for this condition of craziness.

The second vertebra is the seat of diseases of cold and bile. We apply a single application when the person's eyes are yellow, or the area underneath the eyes is yellow, also when the patient has lost his or her appetite. When the disease is, for instance, a problem of not being able to digest food because of a problem of bile, then we apply to three points at the same time. If the person eats food, but then feels like throwing up or does throw up, or a bit of bile comes to the mouth, then in these cases one applies three points at the same time.

Going down to the third vertebra, this is the seat for diseases of *bad-kan* and cold. We apply one application when the person has a problem of *bad-kan* that will not allow him or her to digest food properly. The patient feels like their body is heavy and kind of falling, it is difficult for the patient to move the body properly. One applies to three points when the disease has spread to the upper part of the body and, because of the problem of *bad-kan*, one is unable to digest food properly and the shoulder and upper part of the body feels heavier than normal.

The fourth vertebra is used when the problem of *rlung* has penetrated the lungs. When this happens and the *rlung* is kind of blowing in the lungs, then one experiences this as if one did not have any *rlung*, it becomes like it is empty. When there is pain the lungs that means that the density of the disease is stronger.

Sometimes the person has localized pain on the right lung or on the left lung, or on the front or on the back. When there is pain, the doctor applies the treatment at three points. In the Tibetan system, about the working of the lungs we say that there are five mothers working and five sons working. The lungs lie around the heart. The lungs at the back of the heart are called the five mothers, around the front they are called the five sons. The fourth vertebra is to treat the mother lung.

The fifth vertebrae, then, is to treat the son lungs. This manifests when we have a problem of *bad-kan* and there is too much catarrh and it is kind of sticky. In that first case, we apply only to one point. When that catarrh has become bluish in color and also smells foul like pus, we apply to three points. When a person has a problem in the lungs which requires an operation in the West, a problem like cancer, then the mother lung can be taken away but not so the son lung. The person cannot survive without the son lung. This is because the tissue of the lungs is very soft, it is full of holes and has no firmness. The mother lung is bigger and stronger than the son lung. The problem is that when one takes away the son lung, there are many connections between the son lung and the vital vein of life. When one cuts this away, many problems develop and the person dies.

Now for the sixth vertebra. This sixth vertebra is the seat of the vein of life. As before, this is useful for the treatment of cases of craziness. Also it is useful for treatment of a person who has compulsion to talk all the time. We apply treatment to three points when the person also loses consciousness. He or she may be talking normally, then the mind becomes faint and the person loses consciousness. It is also for these cases.

At the seventh vertebra, we apply to one point when we have a case where the person has severe palpitations. We can even see the heart moving fast. And also his or her breathing becomes shorter. We apply three points when the person has severe problems getting to sleep and also when the person has severe pain localated in the heart.

Then the eighth vertebra is the seat of problems of the liver. What are the problems with the liver? We apply to one point when the problem is of weak liver, a liver without strength, or when the liver has been invaded by phlegm, or *bad-kan*. Then a person receives treatment at the three points of the eighth vertebra when he or she has a problem of the liver and becomes thin, or when the person has lost his or her appetite.

The ninth vertebra is connected to the eighth vertebra and has the same kind of response. This is used when the person has a problem of burping and belching whether he or she eats or does not eat. We apply three points when, on top of the first disturbance, the person also has localized pain in the liver whether the person walks or sits. When the liver is aching, then one applies three points.

The tenth vertebra is the seat of bile, the gall bladder disease. For the second vertebra we also said bile, but that is connected to cold. In this one, the tenth vertebra, this is connected to heat. This vertebra is used for the treatment of stones in the gall bladder. In the West, usually the treatment is to take away the stones, but in Tibetan medicine when we apply moxa or needle treatment with heat so the stones dissolve. Then the gall bladder continues to function properly. If the stone is very big, then you apply at three points. If the person has a strong headache, a migraine, and when he or she spits brown bile, and the eyes are yellow, then we also apply three points.

The eleventh vertebra is the seat of problems with the spleen. One applies at one point when the patient reports pain in the spleen and also when the stomach bloats. We apply three points when the spleen creates a sound in the stomach that comes from its disturbance. Usually the person does not have strength and sleeps a lot, then we apply three points.

The twelfth vertebra is the seat of the stomach. One applies one point when there is a problem of warmth, of heat, for digestion, when the food does not digest well. Three points are applied on when the problem is stronger than before. It depends on if there is vomiting, diarrhea, or if the food does not digest at all and remains a hard ball in the stomach.

The thirteenth vertebra is the seat of the seminal vessels. In the case of a woman, then this vertebra is the seat of the uterus. One treats with one point when the woman's menstrual blood has stopped, or her menstruation has a constant flow that cannot be stopped. Also, when she has some hard growth in the uterus. In the case of a man, he is treated here when the sperm or life-quality of the semen loses its potency as soon as it comes out of the body; the semen dies. One applies three points to a man when his semen has gone rotten, that means it is yellow and it smells foul. With this there is sometimes blood and pus coming out with the semen. One applies three points to a woman at this vertebrae when she has a white discharge or a yellowish discharge, or has blood and pus together in the discharge.

The fourteenth vertebra is the seat of problems in the kidneys. Then, one applies one point when there is a problem of an invasion of *rlung* and the kidneys become cold. One point is also applied when there is localized pain in the kidneys. In the case of a man, one cannot apply three points in this vertebra because this is connected with the testicles and if one applies three points this will create an inability for the man to get an erection later, after the treatment. For a woman one can apply three points, and this is done when the woman cannot bend over and touch the floor without pain, or when she cannot move and is lying on her back because of the pain.

The fifteenth vertebra is the common seat for all the five main organs. The cases of one application is when the person has to, for instance, urinate again and again, or has no control over urination. Then also when it burns while urinating. We apply three points when there is a problem of a woman not being able to conceive. In the case of a man, when his semen does not have that power to procreate then one applies three points and the semen recovers its power. Also, it helps for all problem of the lower part of the body.

The sixteenth vertebra is the seat of the lower part of the abdomen. Moxa should be applied in the protrudence, but never in between. If done so, there is much danger that a vein will be damaged. The moxa is applied until the fire is reddish and the patient begins to draw back because he or she feels that heat.

The sixteenth vertebra is for problems of the intestines or lower abdomen when *rlung* has invaded the intestines. This manifests as different sounds in the stomach. One applies one point for this case.

In this first case this is not a constant symptom; sometimes the stomach bloats and there are some sounds, but other times of the day nothing happens. If this is constant due to the invasion of *rlung*, then one applies three points. Specifically, this is good for the treatment of hemorrhoids, the application to three points.

The seventeenth vertebra is used for the treatment of dysentery. Also, when the intestines have a growth or a tumor that blocks it, or also when the intestine is twisted and tangled. It is the seventeenth vertebra, but we are still on the intestines. The case of a tumor is with three points.

The eighteenth vertebra is the seat of the urinary bladder, then one applies one point when there is a problem of a tumor in the bladder, or also cases or prostrate problems. One applies three points when this case has become chronic and also when there is no warmth.

The nineteenth vertebra is the seat of semen. One applies one point when there is blockage where the semen must come out. If there is a great problem with the semen in the sense that it becomes so intensified that the man is unable to walk, he becomes lame, then one applies three points to this vertebra.

The twentieth vertebra is the seat of the *rlung* that purifies downwards. This happens when the person is all the time expelling gas, he or she cannot control it and it goes even when the person walks. One applies one point of treatment when the legs are numb or the back is numb, it is like continually what we can 'fallen asleep', that feeling. We have talked briefly about all these different points in the vertebrae in which all the problems can be localized, but this is really a limited presentation because there are many connections with different veins and different nerves that a doctor uses in treatment. We have no time and it will only confuse you if we go any further. If one massages each one of these points on the vertebrae with oil and nutmeg, then it is of great benefit. The nutmeg has to be powdered. When you do the massage, you touch the three points. There is no danger when touching the three points like this.

There are also small vertebrae at the end of the spine, but I don't know if you call them vertebrae. There is nothing taught for using them. For the coxae, the last vertebra, massage is very good. One should warm up the oil that has nutmeg in it and then dip cotton wool in the oil and put it on the place. Then massage gently until the oil is absorbed. This will result in that the spine will become straight and also the person will be able to go to sleep easier.

If the problem is a separate one of *rlung*, *mkhris-pa* or *bad-kan*, then one massages only one vertebra. If the problem is a combination, then one works on two. If it is a problem of two combined, this is *ldan-pa*, and one works on two vertebrae. *Dri-pa* is a combination of the three. So three vertebrae are worked on at the same time. One can put three, three, and three; three needles in each vertebrae that one is working on.

The massage should be done on the three vertebrae at the

same time. Massage is not bad; it is always beneficial if you just do it on the points. One should start the massaging in the center of the vertebra and then go out to the other two points. By massage itself, one pacifies the disease. The oil and nutmeg work after the disease is specified, by working on the seven constituents of the body to make them stronger. The lack of strength is usually the result of a certain disease. So one works on this disease, and then restores the strength of the patient.

Since we have just covered the points on the back of the body, I would like to just mention a few points on the front of the body. We cannot deal with all the points in the arms and the legs because we do not have enough time. So, we just talk about the back and the front.

Let us start by the point here in the neck, the point that everyone has. This is used for the treatment of a problem of *bad-kan*, and a problem of saliva in the sense that one cannot swallow anymore. This is for instance very common in the case of throat cancer. Then, it should not be applied at the very, very beginning of the disease. One should apply not directly to the point, but half a thumb—nail's distance on either side of the point. This helps for tumors, when the swallowing has become impeded. Applying at this point is good in the cases of hiccups that do not stop, and also to stop excessive salivation.

Then, the next point is under this depression, there is a shape like a V here. One uses this point to cure a case in which there is pain between the shoulder and the shoulder-blades on each side. Some people have a lot of pain in this part of the body.

Now we have to imagine that each point is down the length of a half-thumb of the patient from one point to the next. There is also a depression there. This point helps something that is very common which is when one lies on the arm and it becomes easily asleep, one cannot lift the arm because there is numbness there and so forth. This can be done with application of moxa, or golden needle, or if one massages this point at the bottom of the trachea, the windpipe, when it connects to the lungs. This is applied in the case of the person who always has dryness in the nose. The nose is connected to the lungs, and the lungs at this point have become weakened. This manifests as dryness in the nose or nostrils. Because of this there is a serum in the lungs that is taking the moisture out. What one accomplishes by applying fire at this point is that the serum dries out and the moisture of the nostrils becomes normal.

The place where the heart is located in the body should be found by taking the distance between the two nipples of the breasts and then finding the middle point. This is applied when one shows an orifice, a hole, in the heart. Because the person has a small hole in the heart, then circulation cannot be done properly. The patient shows this by signs such as the tips of his or her fingers turning blue. When one applies heat there, this normalizes circulation and also heals the wound.

Remember that each of these points is half a thumb-nail downwards. So the next point is to treat cases in which the person is depressed, is very hard on himself or herself all the time, is crying, is fighting with the self.

Then the last point: if we go still one half thumb-nail downwards, then we come to the beginning of the stomach at that last protruding bone there. One applies at this point when the *bad-kan* responsible for mixing the different foods in the stomach is malfunctioning and the stomach cannot digest the food and the liquid properly. One can also do three points in this case. One applies in three points when the person eats food but it stays in the stomach for a time then the person throws up. This is because during the first process the food is being heated, is being warmed up, by the fire accompanying *rlung* and then this mixes improperly with the *bad-kan* responsible for mixing. The food cannot be digested properly and comes out again.

The next point downwards is the abode of tumors. Most of the cancers that are formed in the stomach are formed at this point. The tumor starts to form because there is a problem with the fire accompanying *rlung* and it does not work properly in heating up the food in the stomach. The element of earth and the element of water come together and form a hardened spot that develop into the tumor and then into cancer. Also at this point we can apply treatment of three points; not only will the cancer dissolve, but also the ability of the stomach to assimilate the essential nutrients from the food is restored.

The next point downwards is for a problem of digestion with a lot of gas and where the stomach is quite bloated. This is a common type of problem. (For the different cancers there are many different treatments. This is for the treatment of cancer of the stomach.) This next point is for problems of cold *rlung*. This affects the digestion because the warmth of the stomach is not functioning properly. One applies heat there at that point, and digestion is restored. A different application is also for the person who, when he or she sees food, becomes nauseated.

The next point down is the navel. One does not use the navel exactly as a point, but goes equal distance from the right and the left of it. Again using the measurement of the thumb, one distance up from the navel is where the large intestine is. If one uses this point for treatment, it is a treatment for the large intestine. If there is a large problem in the large intestine, like a tumor, then one applies three points. Each point is separated from the middle by half a thumb's length.

Half a thumb down from the navel is the point for treatment of the intestines. This is for the treatment in cases where cold and *rlung* have invaded the intestines, and the person has problems of diarrhea with white-colored feces no matter what color the food is that he or she has eaten.

Going further down we reach the point of application of three points for the diseases of intestine. This is done when the symptoms are not only that the feces is white, but that it is not constantly loose like diarrhea but it is sometimes loose, sometimes hard and sometimes of different consistencies.

One further measure downwards one reaches the sight of the urinary bladder. When there is a problem that *rlung* has invaded the urinary bladder, in this case *rlung* is like air. It is mostly occupied by air so that there is not sufficient room for urine, and the person has to go continually to the bathroom. For these cases, one applies one point. We apply three points when the person also feels a burning sensation when urinating, when the person feels itching when sensing urination, and also when the urine is reddish and has spots of pus discharged.

In order to locate the point for the liver, one should hold one's own hand to one side of the face, with the fingers touching the ear, and then putting the arm down to the body. That point where the elbow touches the body is the point where the liver is. One uses that point to correct problems of inflated liver, and also liver that has water in it.

Actually there are 72 different points in the whole body where one does one treatment or the other with moxa, or golden needle, or massage. It would be too much to go into all of this. Normally the liver is two ribs above, inside, but when it becomes enlarged then it falls under this. When moxa is applied at that point, then because of the heat the liver contracts. Let us stop here with miscellaneous treatments.

Now we will start with diet and behavior. We can only talk briefly because there is not much time left, but we will set the conditions so that it is like a good omen for me to talk about this.

I have compared the Tibetan classification of nutritional strength that different types of food have and also their effect on the body with the same study that is done in the West. It is quite similar. It is mostly the same in almost all cases.

I will talk about one case where it is different, and this the classification of meats. The basic classification is between the animals that live in dry land and animals that are in the ocean or other wet environments. The third classification is with animals that sometimes live in oceans or rivers and sometimes live on earth. They can live in both places. Some birds can stay in dry places and also stay on water.

I will now speak briefly about the different qualities of the different meats and how they influence problems of *rlung, mkhris-pa* and *bad-kan* and so forth. Meat that is coming from animals that live in dry places is good for the treatment of bile and heat. This because a problem of bile is that there is also too much warmth, so therefore the skin becomes yellow and so forth. So, when one eats this meat, it strengthens and gives more vitality to the body. The meat that comes from these animals on dry land is good for cooling the body, it has the characteristic of cool meat. Meat that comes from animals that live in a wet environment, this meat is considered hot. It is good for the treatment of problems of *rlung* and of *bad-kan*.

The meat from animals that live either in wet parts or on dry lands is good for treatment of the three humors or components of *rlung, mkhris-pa* and *bad-kan*.

Generally speaking, the meat that comes from an animal whose hoof is whole, without any split, is bad for the body. The effect of this meat is that it makes one's intelligence dull. For instance, horse-meat and donkey-meat: one of the effects that these have is that awareness and intelligence becomes dull. Also the effect of this kind of meat is that it can create tumors in the veins.

If one has a burn on the body, and also if there is a problem with serum, waste liquids, then pork is good for that. However, pork is bad if there is a problem of bile or phlegm.

I have talked then a little bit about meat. Let us then talk about milk. Generally speaking, milk is the best food for the body to gain strength, vitality. The best milk in this respect is the milk from the red cow. There are these cows whose skin, eyes, and horns are red. Red can mean reddish brown.

I am talking about Tibetan medical science and I am basing my study, all of my lecture, on Tibet. In Tibet, we do not use chemicals, so what I said before about meat holds for the animals that we have in Tibet. It is good that you examine meat according to their quality.

The milk of this red cow is sweet and tasty, and it also gives vitality to the basic constituents of the body. It brings lustre to the body and hair. Also it can clear imbalance in the *rlung* in the bile. For a man, this milk increases his strength and also his humor.

I will now talk about the common cows that we find here in India and in many other places. These are good for problems in the lungs, when for instance there is a problem like a hole in the lungs, and in the case of the person who does not experience localized pain but has to urinate repeatedly. Boiled and warm milk is good for this patient.

Goat milk is good for breathing problems like asthma and so forth. The milk of a sheep is good for cases of *rlung*. There is also milk from the *dri*, an animal that is found in Tibet which is a cross between a cow and a yak. This milk is very good for marrow and bone problems. In some places people drink milk from horse and donkey and this is good for the lungs, but the problem is that the intelligence becomes dull.

There are many different types of water that have been classified in this system. Generally speaking, we could say that healthy water is water that is free of germs and water that has been hit direct sunlight. There are six kinds of waters described in Tibet, but one of them is the water that has eight qualities. That kind of water also is particularly tasty. this water is found on high mountains and in clean ground. It is water from waterfalls.

Q. Could you say something about diet?
A. For vegetarians, fruit, milk, and cheese is very good! Mushrooms are very good. For vegetarians, all vegetables are considered good except one kind of Chinese spinach. To eat only raw food is not good, but one can balance with eating cooked food also.

For people who have problems of *bad-kan* or acid in the stomach or heartburn, then soya bean is not good for them. White rice is the best. Natural white rice is the best because it smells nice and is easy to digest. The other rices, like red rice and brown rice, are sticky and therefore not good for the stomach. Wheat is good, has good power of nutrition.

There are different kinds of mushrooms in many parts of Tibet. There is milk. The milk from the *dri* is very nutritious for the body, it gives a lot of strength. All dairy produce are abundant in Tibet.

Q. Can Dr. Dolma talk about meditation and behavior?
A. There are three points of behavior. The first is the behavior for the method of obtaining longevity or long life. The second one is to act in accordance with the customs of the world where one lives. The third one is to act in accordance with the dharma.

For the first category, the method for obtaining long life is of observing the diet, the seasons, the way of dressing and to have the right discernment to avoid accidents.

The second one is to live in accordance with the laws of the world. In Tibet there are sixteen basic laws of conduct that one should observe. When these laws are observed, then one avoids accident and disease. If one behaves in a special way, avoids fights so one is not likely to be killed in a fight, and so forth.

The most important of all these sixteen laws or counsels is that one should always take as an example one who has great learning or quality so that one can follow in his or her footsteps. One should also respect elders, one's own parents and others, and to serve them also. For instance, the merchant should always say the truth about his or her products. If the stuff is old then the merchant should say so. If it is one kilo then it should be exactly one kilo and not less. One should not listen to what a person of a bad character has to say. If one is a thief or a murderer or is a bad kind of friend and so forth, one should not follow his or her advice. The next one is not to lie, to instead use speech properly, and not to steal. These are laws to kind of live in accordance with the laws of the world.

I will talk a little bit about living according to the dharma, to religion. The first thing in the morning is to clean one's body, to clean one's place or room. If one does not clean or wash one's face after waking up, then one might feel sleepy and fall asleep again. One clears one's awareness in the morning.

The second thing is, whatever one's religion is, to set motivation or imagine one is making offering. One can imagine, or as in the Buddhist tradition, offering butter lamps, or lights, or flowers.

The third thing is to sit straight and to examine one's actions as far as one can remember in this lifetime, which actions are positive and which actions are negative. When one sees all the positive actions that one has done, then one should contemplate on the fact that this action was done with this body, a human body which is the best kind of form for achieving liberation. Then, rejoicing at the actions, one should feel that even though this has effected the body, there are still many beings in a miserable state and to develop compassion for them. Distribute whatever good actions or karma that one has done for them and the release from their suffering. What one is doing is exchanging what one's good for the beings who suffer. One should then think upon past negative actions and the fact that they will only lead to more suffering. One must think and recite: "Even though I have now acquired this precious human body, I have not been able to use it properly and instead have used it only to accumulate negative actions which can only result in negative consequences. Instead of using it to help other beings, or to help myself, I have been indulging in negative actions. I will turn away from these actions and be pure and positive for other beings as well as for myself." So, this whole point is to fix the motivation, fix the intention of one's actions. If one does this in the morning every single day, then by the strength of this, one's own being will become naturally pure.

The next is that meditation is done on one's own lama, guru, meditational deity, or whatever meditational practice that one is engaged in. For instance, when one does Guru yoga with all kinds of devotion to the lama, then after that the lama dissolves into light, merges with oneself, and one remains in meditation in the state of emptiness without thought.

After that, when one rises from practice, then one should fix strongly the intention that whatever one does is done for the benefit of other beings. One should put aside the habit of working only for oneself all of the time and direct all actions to help and bring happiness to all other beings. Thinking only of oneself is not the best way to start the day. The best way is to continue the motivation of compassion. Actually, what matters most is one's mind is the action done and whether it was positive or negative. Even if one has a lot of money, thoughts of negative actions will not allow one to enjoy them. A person, then, may be able to enjoy having only a little money because his or her mind is at peace.

Q. What is moxabustion?
A. In our system, moxabustion is the application of certain herbs that are burned directly on the skin.

Q. Can you explain about mineral baths and how they are used?
A. We use mineral baths, mineral heat massage and also mineral poultice for acquiring physical health.

Q. Can you explain urine diagnosis?
A. We have many different ways to diagnose by the urine. In Tibetan medicine all diseases can be diagnosed through analyzing the patient's urine. The day before giving urine for analysis, the patient should not eat meat or drink alcohol, or engage in any sexual contact. When the patient makes the urine sample, they should throw away, the first half of the sample. The second half the patient should bring for analysis. The container that is used for collecting the urine should be clean, without any medicinal or perfume smell and no oil. It must be thoroughly clean and dry. The doctor then tests the urine in nine ways.

The first test is smell; for example, if the smell is repulsive then the patient has a heat disease. If the urine has no smell, then the patient has cold disease.

The second test is color. For example, if the urine color is yellow or reddish then the patient has hot disease. If the color is white or bluish, then a cold disease is indicated.

In the third test, the doctor tests the bubbles. For example, if the bubbles are big and come onto the surface like sputum, then a hot disease is indicated. If the urine is stirred and the bubbles disappear at once, then this is a cold disease.

The fourth test is sediment. For example, if the urine has sediment on the surface then a cold disease is indicated. If the sediment is on the bottom, then a hot disease is indicated.

The fifth is the feeling test. The doctors place few drops from the urine in his or her hand and lets it dry. If the dry urine feels soft then a cold disease is present. If it feels rough then a hot disease is indicated.

The sixth test is greasiness. For example, if the urine has grease on the surface then a hot disease is present. If there is no grease on the surface then the patient has a cold disease.

The seventh test is sound. When the urine is gently stirred and it gives the sound of dropping water, then this sound means there is a heat disease. When on stirring there is no clear sound, like curd or yoghurt, then it means there is a cold disease.

The eighth test is color change. One lets the urine sit for one hour. If the color changes into white then a cold disease is indicated. If the color changes into brown then the patient has a hot disease.

The ninth test is more on mixing colors, and this can be used to detect many different diseases.

Q. Could I ask you how can hot and cold be explained in terms of the cause of disease?

A. If you want to know the difference between a cold disease and a hot disease you would have to ask me to teach you for one year. Actually there are 42 different cold diseases and 110 hot diseases as well as 32 nervous or mental diseases.

Q. Is hot and cold the same sort of thing as yin and yang or is that something completely different?

A. It is the same. Only the language is different.
Q. What happens if a patient comes to you with a cut or broken bone?
A. If there are broken bones then we use stone substances.
Q. Is there any religious ceremony involved in the preparation of Tibetan medicines?
A. Definitely. In the *Oral Transmission Tantra* (i.e. the third medical text) that is one of the doctors' main area of study.
Q. Can you explain about the three humors and how they relate to the five elements.
A. The wind element is for rlung diseases. Water and earth are for phlegm. Fire and wood are for bile.
Q. I would like to ask Dr. Dolma about two specific conditions. Firstly can Dr. Dolma cure diabetes in, say, a child who is dependent upon insulin? Secondly can Dr. Dolma cure the lung condition known as primary pulmonary hypertension, for which our medicine has no answer?
A. Actually diabetes has two causes. One is pancreas diabetes. The other is kidney diabetes. If these two causes can be detected, then treatment is easy. For a permanent cure it will take four to five months of continuous medicine.
Q. And that is for someone who has been taking insulin injections?
A. No need for insulin. If the person has been taking the insulin, it should be reduced gradually until it ceases completely. As for your second question, primary pulmonary hypertension can be cured with a combination of eleven ingredients. At first this may be hard to believe. When we first practiced in India, there were also doubts; but after observing our treatments, the news has spread to a lot of people and now we see many Indian patients every day. They believe in our system without our having to advertise.
Q. Can Dr. Dolma tell us about the causes of leukemia? And can she cure it?
A. Basically speaking, it is caused by a weakness of the bone marrow causing a disease of the blood cells. It is an imbalance in the bone

marrow and the blood. If this is not treated, then it becomes leukemia cancer. There are different reasons why this happens. Briefly it is caused by incorrect diet, certain behavior and contact with freezing water.

Q. Youve mentioned curing leukemia though applying acupuncture between the fifth and sixth vertebra.

A. Acupuncture and massage alone can not cure leukemia. It needs medicine. Acupuncture only gives relief, helping the energies to circulate, but it cannot cure by itself. The medicine to be given is a combination of jewelry substances and natural herbs, a formula comprising 25 ingredients in all.

Q. Is there any obvious difference between using herbs in preparation, minerals, or jewels? Is there any obvious thing to separate them?

A. There are different ways of combining substances to be used in medicine. Especially almost all jewels and gem ingredients require purification. First we will look at gold. Gold is a substance of medicine. It is used in medicine to promote long life such as in rejuvenation pills and to cure poisoning. Gold in itself has three types which can be used in medicine. There are other types as well but these three types are used: the first (Tib: *tsoma*) is a brown reddish-yellow. Actually gold is yellow in color but this is slightly reddish. The second is the pure yellow-colored gold. The third is white-colored gold. Used directly, gold is poisonous. Therefore, before using it as medicine it has to be purified.

The method to purify gold is as follows:

1. Make the gold into very fine paper, very thin.
2. The gold is then put between two clay packs or containers.
3. Next it is put into a fire made from wood charcoal, not any other charcoal.
4. The fire is increased by blowing onto it. Not too much burning, just a normal fire.
5. When the clay is first put into the fire it has a normal mud color. When the mud color turns into red, at that time the gold is purified.

6. The clay pack is removed from the fire and allowed to cool.
7. When it is cooled, it is turned out onto a clean plate.
8. The purified gold in the clay packs still looks yellow but when you touch it, it crumbles into a powder. When it is in that form, a powder, it is purified. Of the many jewelry substances used in medicine, only gold is purified in this way.

Q. Does it matter what sort of clay you use?
A. The soil or clay mixed with sand is not good. Sandy mud is not good. It spoils the gold. You must use sticky mud.

Q. When you break the clay container how do you stop the gold from powdering and mixing with the clay?
A. No, it comes away from the clay easily and falls onto the plate. It never sticks to the clay.

The next jewel we would like to consider is opal, famous in Australia. As for the benefits of using opals in medicine, it is said that opal is good as a tonic for all diseases. It is especially good for controlling or preventing the influence of negative or evil spirits. It is a good general cure for all diseases caused by evil or negative spirits. Also turquoise is very good for all liver diseases. It gives the liver energy. It purifies poisons in the liver, cirrhosis of the liver, liver damage, liver cancer and so forth.

Q. And hepatitis?
A. It is very useful in the hepatitis treatment, too.

Q. Does it have a regenerative effect?
A. Yes. Using turquoise in hepatitis medicines has some sort of magical effect. Hepatitis can be cured in a week or two.

Q. Do you have to mix the turquoise with other herbs?
A. Yes, other herbs have to be used.

Now pearl—white pearl is good for the brain, brain damage, weakness in the brain giving paralysis, epilepsy, brain tumor and for balance of the bone marrow.

All three jewels are purified in the same way. There is another substance that is used in the purification of these three, but first it has to purify. It is called *tseza* and is a salt substance. It is not the salt used in food. Actually there are seven slats, for example a brown one is used for digestion problems. *Tseza* is white. To purify it, it has to be fried over a fire until it bubbles and becomes light. When it loses half its weight, it is ready for purifying the jewels.

1. Break the jewelry into pieces and wash in clean cold water three times.
2. Boil the *tseza* and jewelry pieces together in water for two hours. Use one part *Tseza* to five parts jewels. After boiling, throw away the water.
3. There is a small blue flower called *cungochung* that is common in most gardens. Only the flower is used. The jewelry pieces are mixed with flowers and boiled for one hour. After one hour the opal or turquoise turns white. The jewels are now purified and can then be crushed into a powder for use in medicine.

These are only a few examples of how a jewelry is purified for use in Tibetan medicine. Now I would like to explain a little about herbs.

There are thousands and thousands of herbal ingredients, so we will discuss only six. These herbal medicines are called the six 'king' medicines. They act with the six major organs or processes in our body. For the heart, nutmeg is used. For the liver, saffron is used. For the spleen, black cardamom is used. For the kidney, white cardamom is used. *Tsotsa* means life-giving. It is mental energy or thinking power, so if a person cannot control thoughts, clove—not the four pointed one—is given as it is also somewhat effective. *Tsotsa* is not related to any specific organ but can affect all organs. It is more related to the breath or blood. So losing the life energy or *tsotsa* is remedied by giving cloves.

For the lungs there is a substance called *chuan*. There are two types. One is collected from the joints of certain kind of bamboo (*mochuan*). Another type is earth *chuan* (*tsachuan*), which comes from high mountains. You can't get it from lower altitudes. It is produced from the snow. In some places, the wind blows the snow and it collects in the earth where it can not re-melt and remains like milk powder. It is said that the energy of the snow is melted into the earth. It is called *tsachuan*. These two kinds of *chuan* are the 'king medicines' for the lung organs.

These are the six 'king medicines'. Out of the six, two must have their skins peeled; the other four can be taken as a spice without any purifications. Of the cardamoms, only seeds should be used.

To take these substances as a medicine you have to combine them in equal parts. They have to be equal so that the organs they effect remain balanced. For certain ailments they can be taken individually, but generally speaking it is good to take them all together. They are used as a general preventive, as a treatment for disease and also to restore energies.

Q. What is the best way to take them?
A. The best way to take them is to combine them as a powder and take half a teaspoon with lukewarm water, milk or tea. If you have any kind of digestion problem—vomiting, nausea, wind or so forth—then it is best to take it with a hot liquid, any hot liquid. A regular dosage is half a teaspoon in the morning and half a teaspoon in the evening.

I have come from such a far away place like Tibet to this country here, and also you have come here to hear about Tibetan medicine. This all happened because we have karmic connections. It is my karma for me to come here, and your karma for you to come here. And so we met.

I have talked here about Tibetan medicine. You have heard what I have to say. In this way, we have planted a seed that I believe will grow until each one of you will become doctors and heal many hundreds and hundreds of patients. At some point in time, maybe this will happen! If you come, I am willing to give teaching to anyone who really wants to learn about the Tibetan medical system. If you come to me in Dharamsala, I will teach you for one hour each day. So, you are welcome to come, each one of you who wishes to. There will not be any fee for these teachings.